THE WINDS OF
FORTRESS KULA

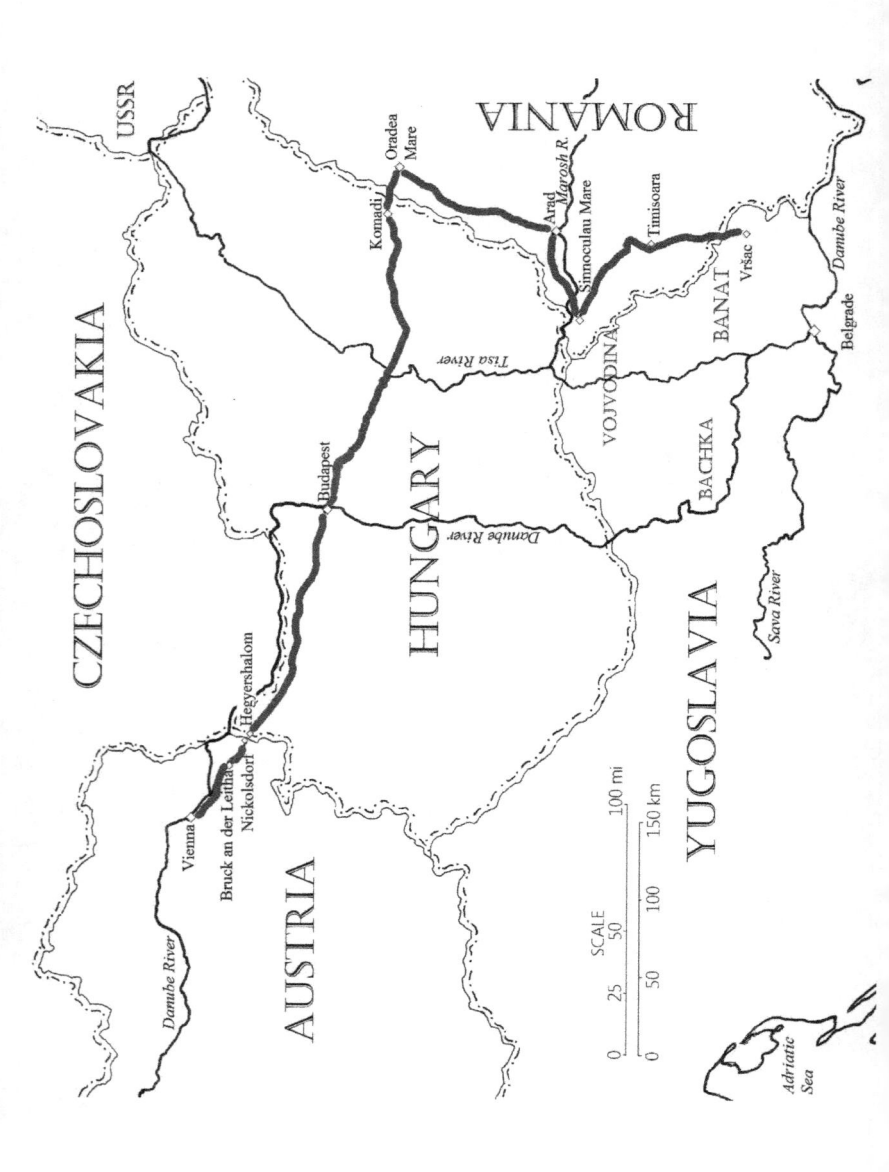

Praise for
The Winds of Fortress Kula

The Winds of Fortress Kula offers Dora Van Vranken's extraordinary account of how she and four siblings escaped from Yugoslav labor camps for displaced, hated and resented ethnic Germans in the cold winter of 1946-47. They struck out on foot for Vienna, hundreds of miles away—and their journey will carry the reader into a powerful personal story, as well as the larger dark realities of post-war Europe. Only fifteen, Dora was the second-youngest among her two sisters and two brothers. Together they encountered many hardships, unpredictable cruelties, as well as kindnesses from the many strangers they would meet. It's a story of a young band of siblings' deprivation, determination, up-and-down luck, courage, religious faith, and most of all, family love and loyalty. You won't put it down.

—Bill McDonald,
PROFESSOR OF ENGLISH, EMERITUS THE JOHNSTON CENTER
OF INTEGRATIVE STUDIES AT THE UNIVERSITY OF REDLANDS

THE WINDS OF FORTRESS KULA

**THE JOURNEY OF A YOUNG WOMAN
FROM CAPTIVITY TO FREEDOM
(1946-1947)**

Dora Van Vranken

 FriesenPress

Suite 300 - 990 Fort St
Victoria, BC, V8V 3K2
Canada

www.friesenpress.com

Copyright © 2018 by Dora Van Vranken
First Edition — 2018

All rights reserved.

No part of this publication may be reproduced in any form, or by any means, electronic or mechanical, including photocopying, recording, or any information browsing, storage, or retrieval system, without permission in writing from FriesenPress.

ISBN
978-1-5255-1029-8 (Hardcover)
978-1-5255-1030-4 (Paperback)
978-1-5255-1031-1 (eBook)

1. BIOGRAPHY & AUTOBIOGRAPHY

Distributed to the trade by The Ingram Book Company

TABLE OF CONTENTS

1
ALONG THE DITCH OR THE POPLAR TREES?

25
TWO WHITE POSTS

45
ONLY A STONE'S THROW AWAY

75
THROUGH A FOREST OF BIRCH TREES

89
UNLUCKY BIRDS

107
THE BLACK, BLACK WITCH

121
"OUT OF THE DEPTHS DO I CRY"

129
A RIVER AND A STAR

155
THE RUSSIAN TRUCK

167
ARE WE IN AUSTRIA?

179
WHAT ELSE?

191
OF TIME, HUNGER, AND OTHER THINGS

217
NOT FORGOTTEN

235
OUTSIDE THE PRISON GATES

For Krista and Nadine

In Memory and Appreciation of my Parents

With Gratitude to the Strangers
who showed us Kindness

On a hazy autumn afternoon some years ago, while sorting through family files and letters, I came across the worn, nondescript little notebook that for years, we feared had been lost.

Overjoyed, I held it in my hands. I noted its smallness, its scuffed edges, the faded color and stains on both front and back covers. I shook my head—it had survived! Between these tan-colored hard covers lay the signposts and proof of our story. It was as if sparse-hewn stone sculptures in an isolated landscape were arising, astonishing me with their presence and reality.

And yet, I was reluctant to open it. Perhaps I feared that what I'd find rising from the pages would revive our experiences in all the voices and colors.

At last, I open the notebook. Faded pencil entries made during our flight, in the distinctive handwriting of my then nineteen-year-old sister, Irmgard, fill the yellowed and sometimes tattered pages. Owing to the book's size as well as to the impulse for secrecy, so natural to fleeing refugees on foreign soil, ever alert to new captors, her script is uncharacteristically small. It is slow reading, but memory comes to my aid, even as the writing supports my memory.

1

ALONG THE DITCH OR THE POPLAR TREES?

The story of our flight begins for me at dusk on the eve of November 18th, 1946 when my older sisters, Hedy (21) and Irmgard (19), and I, Dora (15), walked out of our internment camp with the intention of fleeing over the border into Romania that night with our two brothers.

With our imprisonment by the former Yugoslav communist regime in October 1944, we, like our possessions, had become the property of that government. Farmed out from the central internment camp in our former hometown, Vršac, to a state-run winery, we were among seventy ethnic German women and girls who had been placed in this camp in mid-March for eight months of arduous vineyard work. Once a lovely German-owned villa, surrounded in every direction by acres of vineyards, it had been confiscated by the Serbian communist government—as was all the property of the some 500,000 ethnic German citizens in Yugoslavia. Stripped to its bare floors, windows, and walls, the villa was turned into a labor prison camp for women.

Here, in true egalitarian fashion, we—the daughters and wives from every walk of life and every stratum of society—sat, laid, and slept in crowded proximity on straw that was provided in lieu of cots, chairs, or benches. Our bundles, holding our few possessions—perhaps a second dress, a woolen shawl or cardigan, a set of underwear, a spare pair of socks or stockings, perhaps one or two photos showing us with family members now torn from us (or, in the case of some devout older Catholic women, a rosary along with a picture of a patron saint)—served for some as pillows; which with a sheet, blanket, or coat, made up our beds.

Everyone rose six days a week at the sound of the bugle at predawn, ate the allotted bowl of thin soup and a piece of country or polenta bread, and lined up for the counting of heads. This was followed by our march to an appointed vineyard, often many kilometers away, where everyone was expected to carry out the same strenuous work regardless of age or experience. Side by side between the rows of grape vines, compassion and solidarity might prompt one of the more expert and hardy former farmer or day labor women to step over to the adjoining row to help a struggling peer.

At the end of the ten to eleven hours of work, signaled by a whistle from the overseer—an affable former Swiss wine-grower with an eye for pretty, young girls—we'd start our march back to camp in pairs or single file. Sometimes, one of the more cheerful and robust young women or girls might start up an old, lighthearted or wistful folk song, joined soon by a chorus of voices. This could buoy our spirits and make us forget our weariness and aching bodies. At other times, one of them might initiate a song of recent vintage which had grown from the soil of their own folk-experience: imprisonment, separations from husbands, sons, daughters, brothers, sisters, and parents; loss of home and homeland. Songs so new that few could join in, but which resonated painfully in each of us; the experience of all that had been taken from us.

November had come; the vineyard work was almost completed. The grapes had been harvested, the grapevines cut and bundled, the grape stumps covered with soil to protect them from the coming winter frost. Snow had fallen, preventing us from finishing up our work in the vineyards closest to our camp but giving us the welcome opportunity for some rest and a little leisure.

On the morning of the unseasonal light snowfall, we could see through the front windows of our attic room the stretch of vineyard still awaiting the winter preparation. The grapevines, fanning out from their snow-hooded stumps, were still carrying their faded yellow leaves. Seen from the distance and against the light blanket of snow that would soon give way to melting, the dark vines looked like stalks with frail points of light.

We knew that any day now, we would be transported back to the central camp in town. We dreaded the thought of it. Here at least, we were surrounded by nature, could find comfort, and for moments, refuge and forgetfulness in its beauty. Here we could breathe fresh air and take in the light of the outdoors; could sit in the large, shaded courtyard where in spring, cherry and pear trees bloomed, and in summer, rose hedges sent out their profuse blooms.

The low-roofed city internment camp was dark, gloomy, and overcrowded. Two years of suffering, fear, and despair hung in its air and dripped from the walls of its rooms. Epidemics and the faces of hopelessness and despondency would await us there, with no chance of stepping beyond the closely-guarded perimeter of a single sidewalk surrounding the camp. One consoling thought about returning was to see and possibly be with our mother and two youngest siblings, who were confined there. Since our transfer to this labor camp, our father had been transported to an unknown destination. We were to learn much later that he was, in fact, sent to the notorious internment camp, Rudolfsgnad. Faced with our imminent relocation, we knew with fearful hearts that we must seize the opportunity and escape while still in this camp. Here we could move a little more freely, and we were less tightly-guarded.

The thought of escaping and fleeing across the nearby Romanian border and on to Vienna, Austria, where, as ethnic Germans, we expected to find a safe haven and freedom, was not entirely new to us. Our brother Gerhard's duties in the town winery gave him unprecedented freedom of movement as a prisoner. He had a kind, lenient supervisor who knew him from his pre-internment days, and who liked and trusted him. On his few Sunday visits to our camp, Gerhard had initiated the topic of a joint flight. Much later I learned that he had also broached the subject with our mother.

On the morning of November 18th, our younger brother Eduard (14) unexpectedly turned up at our camp. This was the first time he had come to see us, for he didn't have the same privileges that Gerhard (17) enjoyed. Informed by two women, who had seen Eduard arrive, we were able to have this unreported contact with him in a corner of the courtyard. Eduard's restless and excited face told us at once that he had secretly sneaked out of his camp to bring us an important message. And so it was.

In a hushed, rapid voice, he told us that Gerhard was already in hiding, in order to escape being sent back to the central internment camp the next morning. His defection would be discovered no later than this evening, when he would have to check in at his supervisor's house. This meant that he'd have the last opportunity to flee across the border this very night. If we wanted to flee with Gerhard, as Eduard planned, we'd have to meet them at the home of two women who were underground guides, soon after dark.

"*Ja, wir kommen.*"—*Yes, we will come,* we told Eduard.

"Today is our lucky day; it's Election Day. As we know, they'll be drinking a lot to celebrate," Eduard said with a grin on his face and a meaningful look. We smiled back at him, nodding. Then we hugged him and urged him to hurry back, and to be careful.

"See you tonight. *Juche die Freicheit!*"—*Long live freedom!* he whispered, lifting his cap as if intending to throw it into the air.

With tremors of fear and excitement we waited for the hours to pass, while at the same time, fearing the hour when we would have to act. The plan was laid out by Irmgard: We would choose a moment close to suppertime, shortly before dusk when hopefully the camp guards and the women—including the ten who shared the small attic room with us—would be indoors on this cool, misty, late autumn day, visiting one another and not paying much attention to anything else. We confided our plan to Lene, a girl with whom we had become friendly and who we trusted. She would keep watch over the conditions inside the house, and peer into the room when they seemed favorable. One of us, in turn, would be looking through the attic room windows facing the front yard to see if all was clear outside.

Lene peered into the room and I, standing watch at the windows, nodded at Irmgard and Hedy.

"Let's take a little stroll in the courtyard," Irmgard said in a normal voice so that the two women in the room, bent over their mending, could hear her. We put on our coats and walked out of the room. Earlier, we had put into our pockets our head coverings, gloves, handkerchiefs, toothbrushes and combs. At opportune moments during the day, one or the other had slipped on a second pair of socks, a top, or a skirt. The few other belongings, such as a blanket, were of course left behind in order to avoid arousing suspicion.

With a nod and soft *"Danke"*—*Thank you*—from us, and the victory sign of Lene's cautiously raised hand, we turned and descended the steep, narrow staircase. Halfway down, I looked back—and meeting Lene's eyes, gave a victory sign back. She acknowledged it with a faint nod, as a look of both hope and sadness flitted across her face. We were to learn a few years later that Lene and her mother had managed to escape from one of their subsequent internment camps a year or so after our defection, making it across several borders to their eventual freedom.

Near the foot of the staircase, we were met by the murmur of women's voices coming from back rooms on the ground floor. We hesitated. Through the open doors, we could make out in the pale light of the late afternoon the figures of women—some sitting on their bedding on the floor, bent over mending; others standing with their backs turned to us. Just as we were about to step into the anteroom, we heard male voices starting to sing. We paused. They were coming through half-open French doors. We could see the figures of two males and a female sitting at a table under a dim ceiling light, two rooms away. The singing and guitar playing were intermittently interrupted by laughter.

We exchanged glances, deeming it our good fortune that the jovial voices were those of our two guards, and that the guitar playing was that of our good-hearted fellow prisoner, Mitzi, who had been appointed camp supervisor. The two guards had been in town to cast their vote this morning and had returned shortly after noon to relieve the two other wardens so that they, in turn, could register their vote in town. The joviality, audible in the guards' singing and laughter, bore testimony that they were celebrating with wine and song the certain victory of their leader Josip Tito, well in advance of tallying the vote. His victory was, of course, a foregone conclusion. For any deviation from the party line (a line which was backed up by force, intimidation and favoritism)—whether discovered or even suspected—was certain to invite retribution, ranging from persecution to public humiliation and ridicule.

We opened the door to the glassed-in veranda that stretched along the house front, and walked toward the door leading into the courtyard. We saw no one. A few steps further and we were behind the shrubs and trees enclosing the courtyard in a half-circle. Here, we stood with pounding hearts for seconds, holding our breath as we listened for sounds coming from the villa—and surveyed the wide, long stretch of vineyards before us.

"Nichts, gehen wir!"—Nothing, let's go! Irmgard whispered under her breath.

Hedy and I followed her a few steps closer to the center of the hedge and looked around, listened intently once more, then began to run with backs bent through the rows of the remaining grapevines that hadn't yet been cut back for the coming winter. The rows led from the house all the way down to the country road.

From time to time we would turn our heads and look back to see if someone was coming after us. We would stop and crouch low to catch our breath, listen for a noise we thought we had heard, or look for a shadow we thought we had seen fall on the path right in front of us. "It's the dry grape leaves that rattled as we brushed against them," or, "It's our fear conjuring up ghosts," one or the other would whisper, eliciting from the others a relieved nod and a self-mocking smile.

Pressing forward in this feverish manner, we reached within some twenty minutes the country road leading eastward to Romania, a mere thirty or so kilometers away, and westward to our former hometown Vršac, ten or twelve kilometers away. Still under the protection of the vineyards, we peered in both directions. Nothing was in sight but an old peasant cart drawn slowly by a single, underfed horse with a tired peasant in tattered clothes sitting with his hands atop the reins and the whip across his lap. They were heading toward town, and appeared indifferent to any goings-on.

Alluding to the obvious disparity between proclaimed policies and ideals and the actual practices of the communist party and government, Hedy couldn't resist commenting:

"Well, times apparently didn't get any better for him either and he surely is a Serb or Czech!"

"Yes, and he is obviously not a bourgeois either, one who exploited the working class, but only a poor, small farmer or day laborer," added Irmgard.

It appeared safe, for the moment, to step out of the vineyards and proceed along the highway to town. But should we walk on the side with the ditch along the foot of the vineyards, in which, if need be, one could squat down and hide from view—or on the opposite side, where large, old poplar trees lined the wide walking path next to the highway? We decided that the tree-lined side was probably the safer one to take. The large tree trunks and the shadows their crowns cast promised some protection. Crossing the highway, we turned our steps toward our former hometown. We were walking at a steady pace, but not so fast as to attract attention. The path was familiar to us. We had walked on it a hundred times in the days before our internment: on the way to family outings, when visiting school friends living in villas amongst vineyards or fruit orchards, and right after the war when we could get hardly any food and our parents managed to lease a patch of land a little ways outside of town to grow some vegetables.

Dusk was beginning to give way to the early onset of darkness. Although nervous and conscious of ever-present danger, we felt, nonetheless, excited for having succeeded at what seemed to us the first and major hurdle. Experiencing a foretaste of the freedom we would soon enjoy, feeling almost as if we had regained it already, we smiled—alluding to our escapade in hushed voices and, feeling high-spirited, took each other's arms, laughing under our breath. We kept up a steady pace, ever mindful that every minute counted. By now we may have been discovered missing, which would certainly give rise to the dispatch of a search team.

Soon we saw a half-moon peering through clouds as though through stage curtains, its pale light spreading over the hills and bringing into shadowy relief the remaining tower of the fortress Kula atop the lone, narrow mountain. Home to nesting eagles lifted by spinning winds to circle its jagged walls, the ruin served as an abiding symbol from the times of the Ottoman Turkish raids and wars of survival and victory. Won by dint of sacrifice and endurance, perseverance and ingenuity, it stood there like a remote, dark patron saint.

Eclipsed by patches of clouds, the moonlight was spreading now across the vineyards and country highway, casting broad bands of light and shadow onto our poplar-lined path. We were not yet quite half way to town when a shock like a bolt of lightning went through us. Our eyes caught sight of two male figures approaching us on the ditch side of the highway. Already, we were able to make out first the militia caps they were wearing, then their uniform-like outfits. Were they carrying guns slung over their shoulders? Now we could hear their voices, and make out a few words spoken in Serbian. Looking at the men from the corners of our eyes, we could see that their heads were turned to scrutinize us. Their searching gaze remained on us until we were behind them. They had not called out to stop us, or crossed the highway to look at us more closely before interrogating us; but had continued—after a seemingly palpable hesitation—to walk eastward in the direction of the camp. With trembling knees; placing one foot in front of the other like automatons, not knowing where our power and control had come from—we continued to move westward.

No one spoke. After some time, Irmgard turned her head to make certain no one was behind us, and finally said under her breath what each of us knew:

"Unsere zwei Wächter."—*Our two camp guards.*

"Yes." I confirmed, shuddering. And after a bit: "And how lucky that we weren't on the side of the ditch!"

"That would surely have been the end of us," volunteered Hedy, with a voice that sounded more like it stated a fact than a fear.

Sobered by having been but a hair's breadth away from our undoing; from predictable punishment, torture, and perhaps death, we quickened our steps—eager to reach our former hometown. There was no more bantering. We walked in silence.

After some thirty minutes, we reached the outlying houses of Vršac. As we approached the house of long-time family friends and members of our father's former parish, Irmgard expressed the desire to say hello to someone who knew us; to leave word with someone that we were fleeing across the border that very night, with the hope it would reach our mother—for there was no other way for us to pass on or record information than by word of mouth.

Irmgard knocked on a lit window facing a short, narrow side street, while Hedy and I stood in the shade of a nearby tree. Hesitantly, one part of the window was pushed open from inside, and in the lit-up space appeared the face of Frau Kovaček. Recognizing Irmgard and hearing her speak in German, her face froze with fear. With a gesturing motion, perhaps involuntarily, she shooed her away. But before Frau Kovaček could shut the window, a man stepped behind her, leaned over her shoulder, and said to Irmgard with a quick, hushed voice in precise German that betrayed an educated Serbian speaker: *"Einen Moment, ich komme sofort."*—*One moment, I'm coming right out.* It was Franja, the son of family friends in Belgrade, visiting the Kovačeks. He was well-known to us, as he and his family had stayed at our home for several weeks following the 1941 air raid of Belgrade by the German "Luftwaffe", when their house had been bombed. We had also seen him more recently, for he had visited us in our labor camp on one or two occasions.

15

Walking at Irmgard's side, Franja led us through the dark back streets to the house of the two sisters who were to be our guides. In response to our surprise at finding him at the Kovačeks and, for that matter, in Vršac, he explained that he had come to see if we were still planning to escape. Unable to locate Gerhard, from whom he expected to get the latest word, he had stopped by at Frau Kovaček's in the hope that she might be able to give him some information. He had barely broached the subject when Irmgard knocked on the window.

It had begun to drizzle before we reached the house of our guides. Franja tapped on one of the lit windows.

"Ko je to?"—*Who is this*? a woman's voice asked in Serbian.

"To sam ja, Franja, i sestre od Gerharda.— *It's me, Franja, and Gerhard's sisters.*

He had met the woman once before, when he accompanied Gerhard with the requested money for guiding us to the border. She unlocked and opened the street door, then quickly closed it behind us and locked it again. She ushered us into a dimly lit room, where we saw her older sister; a slighter woman. Both appeared to be in their late thirties or early forties. They greeted us in a reserved manner and invited us to sit down. Their faces were tense and alert, their movements deliberate. Everyone fell into whispering. In a little while, the door to the room was quietly opened and Gerhard stepped in. After many hours hiding in the sisters' attic, Gerhard now blinked as he looked around, blinded by the unaccustomed light. Recognizing us, his face lit up.

"Ihr seid hier!"—*You're here!* he exclaimed, with a smile of relief. The plan was working. We would flee with him across the border tonight. Once again, the excitement over our imminent freedom filled us with joyful anticipation. It seemed ever closer.

The women were looking at their watches, and at Gerhard and Franja. It was time to leave. Where was the fifth? Why was Eduard not here yet? What could be detaining him? Suddenly, our new joy was replaced with frightening thoughts and images. Had he been caught trying to sneak out of his camp, or was it impossible for him to get past his camp guards tonight? Had something happened to him on his way back from our camp? Twelve kilometers, walked probably on back roads in zigzag fashion to avoid detection, was a long way—and anything could happen. Perhaps he couldn't find his way in the dark in this unfamiliar sector of town. Fear and sorrow filled us for our normally so fearless and adventurous younger brother. We looked at each other with dread. How could we leave him behind? And yet, there was no staying; no going back. We were forced to move forward.

Franja, who had been talking with the women,

turned to Gerhard. The two were consulting. It was decided that Franja would go to Eduard's camp and try to get him out. Gerhard knew the camp's location and would lead him to it. But how would Franja manage Eduard's release? He was just a civilian. Surely the guards wouldn't hand over a prisoner under their care without a written order or an oral permission from their superiors.

"We'll have to try and do what we can," responded Franja with a pale smile. "God works wonders. And look at me," he said as he stood up the collar of his black leather coat, tightened his belt and assumed a humorously authoritative pose, while reaching with his hand to the inside of his coat as though reaching for something from a pocket of his coat lining or jacket. Switching to a regretful mien, he pointed to his rather soft leather shoes, as if to say, too bad that I'm not also wearing polished, stiff boots. For a brief moment we all laughed under our breath. Even the two women couldn't help snickering at this witty performance.

As Franja and Gerhard slipped out into the night, we could hear the sound of gentle but steady rain. I involuntarily raised my shoulders and drew in my neck, as if already feeling the cold wetness coming down on me during the impending march through the dark streets and fields, and the crossing of the border.

With fervent thoughts, we besought the heavens for their assistance to this mischievous, adventurous brother of ours, whom we had nicknamed Puka. On the morning of our first internment, October 5th, 1944, he had remembered to run up to the attic and open the window of the dovecot to release the pigeons, while the militiamen in our courtyard were already impatiently calling for our family of nine to hurry and get going and join our "Švabice" neighbors at the street corner. And then the sudden flapping, whirring sound of two dozen wings emerging from a window on the house roof: a light gray cloud diving, then rising, and taking off across the sky. And there was Eduard emerging from the attic, his eyes smiling.

With their heads close together, Irmgard and Hedy were speaking in a low voice; Irmgard filling in Hedy on what she had learned from Gerhard. I caught her saying "Mama" and then, *"Sie hat sagen lassen, sie kann nicht. . ."*—*She sent word that she can't.* And the names—"Mama!. . . Claudi!. . .Waldemar!"—We were leaving them! They were right here in town and we wouldn't see them. We were leaving tonight and might never again see them! And what if they'll be punished for our defection?

"No!" I wanted to shout, "We can't leave them behind and abandon them to their fate!" Terrified, I looked at my sisters, as if to mobilize their help. They too looked troubled, as if in the grip of these wrenching thoughts. I turned my glance downward again and remained silent.

As captives and dispossessed, young and old alike, we had learned to be silent about our deepest fears, sorrows, and longings. Everyone had losses, separations, and dreads. No one could alter that, neither for himself nor for the other. We didn't speak about these things, not even to a sister or brother, and much less to a parent. For we knew that parents suffered not only their own fate but also the fate of their children. To a friend in prison camp one might sometimes speak of the way things used to be, almost as if trying to tell them who you were.

I could see before me my mother's face again as I had seen it several weeks before. On the chance of a visit with her after our six-month separation, I feigned a painful wisdom tooth to the camp authorities in the hope that I might be allowed to join five older women from our camp, who would be taken to town for the extraction of some of their painful cavity-ridden and broken teeth. Fillings were no option, of course. As I had hoped, following the dentist's prolonged extractions which lasted late into the evening, we were put up for the night in the central internment camp in town, where my mother and the two youngest siblings were confined.

I told her that we five sisters and brothers planned to escape from our camps and flee over the border to Romania, with Vienna as our goal. I saw her face turn pale—frightened, and unspeakably sad. Her lips trembled as I met the full gaze of her large gray-green eyes. They seemed even larger for the deepened pallor of her face, and its now-visible bone structure. She took my face between her hands, and drawing it closer to hers, said:

"Ja, geht ihr habt meinen Segen."—*Yes, go, you have my blessings.*

Shivers were running through her thin body. Expressing my hope that she and my two siblings would not be subject to any retribution on our account, she looked down at our four-year-old brother, Waldemar, who was sleeping peacefully next to us on the floor on a pile of straw with a sheet spread over it—and nodded. She kept nodding, and remained without reproach by either look or word.

And Claudi! I can still see the face of our lovely twelve-year-old willowy sister as she responded with a look of shock and fear, which gently gave way to a smile, reflecting her guileless sweetness as she looked into my eyes.

The expressions on their faces will always pierce

me, will never cease to astonish me. I ask about their source, I marvel about their existence.

It was one thing to leave our mother, sister and brother. In contrast, leaving Vršac was not difficult. The place where we had grown up, had gone to kindergarten and school, had been happy as a family, had had friends and neighbors, streets and trees we loved—all this was ripped from us and forever changed by the terrifying noise of machine guns that sunny October Saturday, followed by the appearance of the blood of 123 Danube Swabians (including farmers and day laborers plucked from their farm carts and from country roads; one widow, and her 11-year-old son) snaking its way down the gutter of our street. And in the silence that finally followed, there was the echo of the procession of cartwheels over the cobblestones as wild-eyed horses cowered, turning onto the dirt country road, now carrying human cargo to the city *"Schinderhaufen";* the dump for animal cadavers. Imprisonment, loss of our civic rights and possessions, separation from our family, forced labor, hardships, intimidations and cruelties, strangers living in our house and with our things—all this had long ago cut the ties that had once bound us to our town and country. Hope, life, and a future lay beyond the borders.

There was a tapping on the guides' window. Everyone's eyes were fixed on the younger of the two sisters who peered through the crack of the opened windowpane. We saw her nod.

"They are here," she said, turning to us, visibly relieved. When she returned to the room with Franja, Puka, and Gerhard, we looked at the three with disbelief and excitement. Their faces looked pale from strain and exhaustion. But they were smiling. Crowding around them, we asked with amazement how they had managed.

"He posed as an agent of the secret police," explained Eduard with an excited and meaningful look.

With a short, nervous laugh, while brushing with the back of his hand past his brow as if to wipe off some perspiration, Franja said, "Yes, and Puka almost spoiled it and delivered me into the hands of the secret police."

All further accounting was cut short, as the two women, now in their dark coats and head covers, were pressing for our departure. It was time we left.

I can't remember leaving the house or what I, or any of my sisters and brothers may have said to Franja, or what his parting words were to us. I am certain that we each thanked him. He not only had retrieved Eduard at great personal risk, thus taking from us the excruciating burden of having to leave without him, but had also come up with the 3,000 dinars—money that we, of course, didn't have—to pay our guides. And I am certain that Franja, in turn, wished us success and God's protection.

Family on a hike in the hills near Vršac, 1940. Left to right, front row: Eduard, Claudia, Gerhard. Back row: Hedy, Sister Francis, Mama, Tata (Father), Erika, Dora (the author), Irmgard.

2

TWO WHITE POSTS

I see us stepping out into the night and walking along a dark, unlit, narrow street, with newly-buoyed spirits and a keen sense of the momentum of the hour. I can see the two dark figures of our women guides at the head, followed by a sister and brother a little distance ahead of me, and another sister walking by my side. The fifth in our group—probably Eduard—brought up the tail of the huddled-up retinue. The rain fell in a steady downpour. Soon, all whisperings and exchanges stopped. With bent heads, holding our coat collars together, from time to time pulling our head coverings deeper over our foreheads to keep the rain out of our faces, we walked with a single focus on our goal.

I see us leaving the last of the scattered, small houses behind and turning, after some dozen yards, onto a dirt road. I remember glancing back once more at the tiny human dwellings as we moved into the black night before us. Heavy rain and dense, low clouds eclipsed the moonlight. Puddles of dark water dotted the dirt road. The wet fields shimmered and glistened. No words. Only the falling rain filled the silence.

Irmgard writes in her account that we had put some sixteen kilometers behind us when the women switched course, turning from the country road and taking us diagonally across the fields. I, too, remember this shift in direction and how it at once put us on the alert. The women looked serious and tense. The air felt charged with danger. We knew that the border was close. Soon, we saw a light in the distance.

"The border patrol hut!" our guide whispered.

As we came closer, we could make out a white, cube-like hut. From its single, square window, bright light was pouring out into the night as if its purpose was to be a lighthouse. Our hearts were in our throats. Shortly, the woman gave us a signal. We stopped and crouched. She pointed with her outstretched arm to the right of the border patrol hut, and we now saw two white posts gleaming palely in the darkness.

"That's the border. Pass to the right of the posts and then run forward!"

Startled and frightened, we looked at her as we suddenly realized that our guides would not take us over to the other side. We would have to venture into the lion's den by ourselves.

"They won't be coming out into this God-forsaken night," she tried to reassure us.

"Idite sada, idite!"—*Go now, go!* she urged in Serbian. With a voice that betrayed feeling and compassion, she whispered, *"Sa srećom! Neka bog bude sa vama, deco!"*— *Good luck! God be with you, children!*

We thanked them and then ran, hunched over, with Gerhard in the lead, careful not to skid on the wet, slippery ground. We reached the posts and continued to run feverishly; to get beyond the sight and the reach of the border patrol whose sense of duty, we feared, could still have been persuading them to survey the nightly scene. Finally, we stopped to catch our breath. Crouching, we turned our heads and looked back. There was no one in sight. The posts were no longer visible— the border hut appeared as a speck in the dark. We looked at each other. Smiles slowly rose on our faces. Relief and joy welled up inside us. We began to laugh and stammer:

"Wir haben's geschafft! Wir sind in Rumänien! Wir sind frei!" We've made it! We're in Romania! We're free! We were jubilant.

"Wasn't that some border," our younger brother, always ready to make jokes, observed with curled, mocking lips. "Two ordinary posts and the same mud on both sides. You'd think that with all that fuss there'd be something impressive about it, but no, the same fields, dirt, and mud," he said, looking from one of us to the other with his quick, eagle-like eyes. We nodded in agreement. We each had had the same thought go through our minds.

Rising to our feet and drawing close with our arms around each other's backs and our heads touching, we stood in silence; each echoing in their heart Gerhard's words of thanksgiving. If someone had seen us from a distance in the dark, we might have been taken for harvested bundles of wheat shafts or corn stalks, stood up for drying and later overlooked and forgotten.

There was no time to linger. We had to move on; find a Romanian farm or village where we might find shelter for the night, as well as reassurance that we were safe and beyond the reach of captors—for we were still close to the border. Our camp guards could still be galloping along its stretches, looking for us. They might have alerted the Romanian patrol, and together with them be hunting us down.

We resumed our trek across the fields. Keeping up the pace was becoming difficult, especially for Eduard and me, the two youngest. We began to fall behind, causing the others to stop and wait till we caught up with them. Sinking ankle-deep into the rain-drenched field soil was tiring, and slowed us down. From time to time, Hedy's feet would get stuck in the mud and Gerhard would have to come to her rescue; retrieve one of her shoes while she, standing on one foot, would lean against him until he had pulled it out and she could slip it on again. Unlike the rest of us, our oldest sister didn't wear high lace-up shoes or oxfords that stayed on one's feet even when one had to pull them out of eight inches of clenching mud. These were the worn-down shoes that we had on our feet the day we walked out of our home to join the march of some 12,000 fellow ethnic German citizens through the city streets to our unknown fate: our first internment camp.

Hoping to come across a road or a signpost, or to espy a church steeple somewhere in the dark that might tell us where we were or in which direction we must go, we were pushing forward in a zigzag fashion—but in vain. The thought that we might be inadvertently re-entering Yugoslavian territory worried Irmgard and Gerhard. Despite their innate good sense of direction, their efforts were of no avail.

At last we stopped. Gerhard slowly scanned the full circle of the nightly horizon. His perplexed look told us that the night had rendered him no clue. He and Irmgard consulted with each other, and scrutinized repeatedly the dark, rain-veiled surroundings. They shook their heads. There was nothing to indicate which course would keep us eastbound. There were no stars, no moon, and no sky in the silent, black space surrounding us. And we had no compass.

Helplessly, we stood in this impenetrable, vast expanse, inundated by the ceaseless downpour of rain and the splashes it made on the dark shimmering pools studding the ground around us like craters in a moonscape. Standing there, feeling the rain running down our faces and its cold wetness seeping through our winter coats and dresses, I for the first time, grasped and tasted our homelessness and forsakenness, which sent shudders through my soul and body.

Whether on faith, intuition, or reasoning, Gerhard and Irmgard decided we should steer in what they hoped was northeast. So we resumed our trek across the muddy meadows and rain-sodden fields. Our pace was slackening. Eduard and I were falling behind more and more often. Hedy was doing only slightly better. Soon Eduard and I began to plead with Gerhard to let us sit down and sleep.

"Just for five minutes," we would beg.

"When we're a little further from the border," Gerhard would say. "When we come across some brushwood where you can sit down," he'd promise later. And when we did stumble on a fallen, half-decomposed tree trunk and later, a pile of cornstalks, we fell asleep the minute we sat down—only to be shaken awake as quickly. I remember us begging with chattering teeth and sleep-drunk, delirious voices to please, please allow us to sleep for only five more minutes.

"It's raining, all of us are wet and cold, we'll be getting ill if we don't move. We must find a shelter to get warm and rest and get our clothes to dry a bit," Gerhard would reason, standing with Irmgard and Hedy in front of us, half-shielding us from rain and wind and smiling benignly, while Irmgard and Hedy were nodding in agreement and looking at us pityingly. Hedy's face was reflecting already the pain she was feeling in her back and legs that would become worse with the continuing exertion, wetness, and cold. And so Puka and I would get up and continue our march through the night.

From the seeming oblivion of the remainder of that first, long night, a few snapshot images, not so unlike memorial stations on roadsides, have remained with me: a field hut, dogs barking, a church steeple, a country road, a road sign, a bridge, church bells chiming the third hour.

Staggering along, sleep-drunk and weary, I remember seeing through the night haze a small structure off a ways in the field. Puka had spotted it and called out:

"Eine Hütte, Gerhard, schau dort!"—*A hut, Gerhard, look over there.*

Eagerly, we had run to it—only to find ourselves bitterly disappointed by its inhospitable condition: missing boards from its roof, leaning, broken sides, mud puddles on the ground. For an instant, the thought of crouching down and leaning against the walls, no matter how porous and unstable they were, seemed infinitely sweet to me. But the three eldest ruled that we should stay out.

We had been back on what we hoped was our northeast trek, pressing steadily if slowly forward. The downpour had subsided. The night air was becoming ever colder. All of a sudden we heard the resounding bark of a dog, joined by another. We stood still. The look of alarm on our faces relaxed. Notwithstanding the shrill edge of the barking, we took the close proximity of the dogs as a positive omen. Perhaps there was a human habitat; a nearby farm or village. Steering now in their direction, we considered shelter in a hayloft or stable. I could already imagine dropping onto the straw and burrowing in for warmth and sleep, when the barking suddenly ceased. We continued in this direction.

As if breaking into my sleep, I could hear Irmgard and Gerhard's joyful voices calling out:

"*Schaut, ein Kirchturm!*"—*Look, a church steeple!* It shone palely in the distance against the night sky. Taking it as our guiding star, we now shifted toward it. It signaled a community and thus, at long last, a place to rest.

Irmgard records that soon after turning our steps in the direction of the tower, we came onto a country road that we gladly exchanged for the fields, despite the greater risks of detection. Not only would walking here be less strenuous; a road post could tell us where we were. And indeed, we were not disappointed.

Soon, we stood before a white road post. Gerhard read out loud the black script on it. Irmgard recognized the village name as sounding Romanian, and Hedy nodded in agreement. Turning to us, Gerhard slowly lifted his cap and declared with a bright grin on his weary face:

"Wir sind jetzt wirklich in Rumänien."—We really are in Romania now.

We embraced each other and did a few dance steps. With interlocked arms, pressing close to each other for joy as well as support and body warmth, we walked toward the tower. The number of kilometers to it did not faze us. Hope once again overrode our weariness and coldness. The steeple loomed ever larger.

Coming out briefly from my drowsy, semi-asleep state, I heard Gerhard talking with Irmgard about what we'd do once we got to the village. Based on this long night's experience, they expected to reach the village around seven. We would first try to find shelter with some farmers, and if not successful, look for a room in an inn. We were aware that this region, like ours, was heavily settled with ethnic Germans. Until the end of World War I, it had in fact been part of our home province, Banat; formerly an outpost of the

Austro-Hungarian Empire. Hearing my two siblings speak, I wondered to myself if the ethnic Germans here hadn't met with the same fate as those in our region had. And how would we manage to get a room in an inn without money? But feeling too tired to ask, I let the matter rest.

I saw a single span bridge above the road. We were standing looking at the road going under and beyond the bridge as through a gateway. Was I imagining a village at the end of the road? It was still dark. The higher banks gave some protection from the wind sweeping across the flat, open land. A deep sound began to vibrate through the silence. The bells in the church tower were gathering momentum to chime the hours in slow, weighty tones. We listened, with every nerve anxiously strained on each chime: One. . . Two. . . Three. . .

We were stunned. How could it be that by the clock's measure, this long, long night had lasted only five or six hours?

We remained by the bridge until dawn, not wishing to disturb the sleep of the villagers. In consideration of the freezing temperatures and our wet clothes, Gerhard insisted that we keep walking to and fro near and under the sheltering bridge till daybreak. Again, we walked in a solitary row, Gerhard and Irmgard on either side of Hedy, whose knees and back threatened to give out.

It was daybreak—a foggy, cold morning with hoarfrost on the banks and ground. It was still early, and the light was that pale gray that seemed so unlike the harbinger of the day; its ashen, equivocal specter calling forth shudders, as if one had unexpectedly come upon shadows of some cosmic evil before its retreat from light into the underworld.

I must have shut my eyes to this ghastly interregnum and given way to sleepwalking. The next scene I saw was wrapped in the first, hesitant blush of winter sunlight breaking through the haze. The seventh chime from the church tower faded away, its sound still reverberating as in a chamber.

We felt excited and hopeful. The morning had come, and with it, the promise of warmth and rest. Alluding to the earlier field hut, Puka speaks of our night's encounter as with a *Fata Morgana* mirage, which makes us burst into short laughter despite being bleary-eyed and stiff with cold. Irmgard and Gerhard were about to set out for the village to find someone who would put us up for a day and night. Our expectations were modest: a stable or hayloft would seem heaven.

"Stay here—don't go anywhere, and be on the alert!" Gerhard advised us, looking hard at Puka who had already run up the banks more than once to survey the surroundings, as well as the bridge.

"Don't stay away too long, come back soon!" we begged them in turn.

"As soon as we have found something," Irmgard and Gerhard reassured us with a faint smile on their tired faces.

I must have sat down at the foot of the bank beyond the bridge and fallen asleep for a while. When I woke up, there was sunny winter morning light all around me. I felt joy rising inside me. Puka was lying near me, eyes closed, soaking up the first morning sun. Hedy was walking slowly back and forth on the road.

"This bit of winter sun does feel good," she said, glancing over with a faint smile that betrayed that she was in pain. "If only the clothes weren't so wet!" The wetness bothered her even more than it did us. As a young child she had accidentally drunk lime and thereby contracted rickets, which left her with a weakened back and bones, and susceptible to pain. With her knees stiffened from the rain, cold, and exertion of the night, she walked as if on stilts; which made her look even taller. She had taken her wet scarf off her head and was holding it out to dry. Light gusts of wind lifted her strong, black, shoulder-length wavy hair.

I wrung my thick braids, which fell well below my waist. My hair was light brown. Not so long before, it had been almost blonde. We all had dark eyes from our father, whose ancestors had come from Alsace-Lorraine.

But Irmgard's eyes were lighter. They were a hazel color, which seemed to have come from our mother—she had gray-green eyes.

"Well, he's back already—and without Igat", Hedy called out while pointing her head in the direction of the road beyond the bridge. Igat was Irmgard's nickname.

Puka was on his feet at once and down the bank, looking expectantly toward Gerhard, who was just stepping out from under the bridge. Although his happy face conveyed good news, we still asked him excitedly,

"Did you find something?"

"Yes, we were lucky. Come on, it's not far from here. The first door we knocked on. Igat stayed with them."

"Volksdeutsche?"—Ethnic Germans?

"Yes, ethnic German farmers, very friendly people."

Igat no sooner touched on our situation with a few words, when the farmers invited us into their home—they didn't even hesitate.

"Come on, let's go!" Gerhard said, rubbing his hands in anticipation or from the cold. We quickly brushed down our damp, crumpled coats, stamped our feet in the hope of shaking off some of the caked mud, replaced our head covers, and set out in pairs toward the village.

Soon we spied a cluster of houses. Smoke was rising from their chimneys into the cold morning air. Gerhard stopped in front of a whitewashed stucco house with three windows, each dressed with impeccable white, starched curtains with simple, handmade lace insets. An extended wall, the height and color of the house, made for a long house front and low-roofed look.

Gerhard knocked on a window. A man's face, looking no older than early forties, appeared between the parted curtains. Nodding and motioning toward his left, the man closed the curtains again. The street door opened, and with a generous motion, the young farmer invited us in.

"Ja, ja, kommt's nur alle 'rein!"—*Yes, yes, just come in, all of you!*

He spoke the welcoming words in a low voice, and upon closing the door, pushed a large bolt across it. I at once felt that he was taking a risk by letting us in.

"Kommt's, kommt's!"—*Come on, come on!* he was saying, motioning us into the house. Looking down at our coats and shoes, we hesitated. Gerhard assured him that we would be grateful to be given cover in his barn. We looked at the barn and hayloft at the end of the large, neatly-raked farmyard.

"Never mind, just come in—it's warm inside, it's all right," the farmer urged in his Swabian-colored German. As we turned toward the house, the door opened. A woman stood in the doorway. Smiling a welcome, she invited us to come in quickly, reminding us that our sister was already inside waiting for us. The woman was dressed in a peasant costume, familiar to me from those worn by the tradition-abiding German farm wives and daughters in our home province, especially in villages.

Scraping our shoes conscientiously on the doormat, we shyly entered the kitchen. It was warm and homey. The wood floorboards, scrubbed clean to an ashen white, were covered with colorful braided rugs. A table stood in the corner; its carved corner benches divided the eating and living area from the kitchen. A large, green-tile stove with benches on its sides radiated a steady flow of warmth. On the black wood stove, steaming pots smelled of porridge. Irmgard, looking warm in her dress, introduced us.

Admiring my long, braids the woman observed, "You can't be older than thirteen."

"I'm fifteen," I said.

"Well, then you're one year older than our daughter Resi. She's with her grandparents for a visit." The woman had that peasant Madonna face one often encountered amongst regional ethnic German farmers; the so-called "Danube Swabian" population of our region: a calm, white face with even features and quiet, brown eyes between two deep folds of a starched cornflower blue kerchief, tied neatly under the chin. The kerchief gave the face a slightly triangular or heart-shaped look, evoking images of old wood sculptures and paintings.

"Come, please sit down. Your sister has already set the table and the porridge is done," she urged after having invited us to take off our coats and put them on the benches by the tiled stove. She ladled out seven bowls of hot porridge from a large, steaming pot by her seat. A brown pitcher with warm milk was passed around, along with a jar of quince jelly for sweetening.

Irmgard had earlier filled in the couple on our story as refugees while Gerhard was fetching us. Sitting around the table, our empathetic hosts inquired about this and that, while looking from one to the other and shaking their heads:

"So young and gone through so much already. And the poor parents, how hard it must be for them, I can well imagine. And in addition, the two little ones—!" the woman said sympathetically.

Her husband, looking serious and thoughtful, observed: "So that's how they've treated their *"Volksdeitsche"* (ethnic Germans). "We did, of course, hear some rumors, but this..."

Gerhard asked if all the ethnic Germans in Romania were still free and in possession of their houses and property.

"So far, they've left us more or less in peace. To be sure, many had some of their fields confiscated by the state. And most farmers have to deliver some of their harvest to the state, and there have been stories of camps and imprisonments in some places in the country as well as transports of young women and men to forced labor camps in Russia. We are sometimes a little afraid. One wonders—communism and so on—but so far, thank God. . ." After a moment of silence he queried:

"Also alle Deitsche, egal ob sie Nazis warn oder net, reich oder arm, jung oder alt? Was denkt's, warum ohne Ricksicht. . . einfach. . ."—"*So, all ethnic Germans, regardless of whether they were Nazis or not, rich or poor, young or old? What do you think, why indiscriminately. . . simply. . .*"

"Ja, alle,"—*Yes, everybody*, Gerhard answered. Shrugging his shoulders and raising his eyebrows, Gerhard suggested that the reason was undoubtedly in response to what the German military, with the cooperation of some ethnic Germans, had done to the Yugoslav Jews and the Serbs. And moreover, the Serbs didn't forget the warm reception the invading Nazi military got in some places by crowds of their fellow German citizens. To them, this was a form of betrayal. Supporting his explanation, Irmgard pointed out that, as rumor had it, the organizing mind in Belgrade behind the disownment and internment of Yugoslavia's ethnic Germans in the fall of 1944 was a communist named Mosche Pijade. The slogan: "Their death not by gas, but by sickness and starvation" was attributed to him.

Everyone was silent.

Gerhard's appraisal was that of our parents and family. Implicit in it was perhaps the unquestioned notion of communal responsibility, by virtue of shared ethnicity if not by incrimination. Our father's known critical view of Nazism and his refusal to join the local German nationalist party —the "Kulturbund"—had not been without certain repercussions for him and the family. That there were also certain religious beliefs underpinning our acceptance and attitude toward our fate, some of us would only come to realize later. But it is true also that we didn't yet know the full magnitude of the suffering and cruelties inflicted upon the entire Danube Swabian population, nor had we become cognizant that its demise was not entirely the direct consequence of perpetrated wrongs, but was in good part the programmatic realization of certain Serbian nationalist intentions that pre-dated World War II.

I opened my eyes. It was dusk. The sense of comfort was astonishing: warm underneath a thick feather quilt, head sunk in a large feather pillow, lying between cotton linens with red stripes. Irmgard, with open eyes, lay to my right. Hedy, to my left, was still asleep. Irmgard smiled at me and whispered:

"Almost unbelievable, isn't it? In a bed, warm and safe and in Romania."

"Yes, and how good that it isn't just a dream," I responded, squeezing her hand that lay next to mine. I raised my head to peek over the high feather quilt. Gerhard and Puka lay in a narrow bed against a wall. They were sleeping on their sides with their legs and arms pulled up, as if still trying to get warm. There was a knock on the door. The woman was calling us for supper. Gerhard woke up.

"What, it's evening? Is it possible that we slept through the entire day?" We all shared his surprise, for we had slept so deeply that we had no sense of the passage of time.

"What do you think about these beds and quilts?" Puka asked with a smile.

"A lot better than that field hut," Hedy responded, her voice muffled by the voluminous cover.

"Yes, and if we'd stayed there, we might never have found our way to this place," reflected Gerhard. Sitting up and sniffing the air, Puka declared that he could smell something good cooking in the kitchen, and that he was hungry.

"Already? So soon?" teased Hedy.

"He's a growing boy, after all", offered Irmgard in a benign voice. As we were leaving the room, she tapped his shoulder and whispered a reminder:

"Please behave yourself at the table. We're refugees and guests, after all."

"No need to worry. You had better tell Dori", he retorted.

"Well, about her I don't need to worry."

A large steaming pot stood in the center of the table, and by the farmer's plate was a round board with a loaf of home-baked bread. Coming to the table, the woman placed a wide bowl with steaming hot dumplings next to the pot. Our hosts had sacrificed one of their chickens for the occasion "to fortify the hungry, fugitive children with a nourishing chicken stew for their long road ahead."

I do not believe that the farmer woman had to attend to any leftovers that night. If we sisters showed self-restraint and desisted because of shyness from accepting seconds or thirds, our brothers did not.

Romania

3

ONLY A STONE'S THROW AWAY

Soon after having risen from our second long stretch of sleep in less than twenty-four hours, and fortified with breakfast, we took leave of our kind hosts.

Never was there more gratitude felt. Gerhard offered them a valuable old silver coin as a token of our appreciation. They refused to accept it, insisting that it might come in handy in a future emergency. With their good wishes and the farmer's detailed instructions to our next stop, we slipped out their street door. To avoid drawing attention to ourselves as a group, we paired up and walked with some distance from each other through the village, returning to the road by which we had entered it on the previous morning. That morning, like the night preceding it, seemed already quite distant.

The country was now covered with a blanket of snow. The air was still and crisp. Our breath curled like steam in the icy air. It didn't faze us, for we were in a confident and expectant mood.

Once on the road, Irmgard asked Gerhard if he had managed to leave the silver coin with the couple after all. Yes, he had gone back to the bedroom on some pretext and left it with a note where it couldn't be overlooked. We all felt glad.

"Gerhard, how did you get that silver coin?" Puka finally asked.

"That's a story only I know." Gerhard answered.

"Do you have more of them?"

"For emergencies." was Gerhard's succinct response, as he switched to the day's plan. No one thought of the silver coins again until a shift in our fortunes a few days later.

Meanwhile, we were rested, physically and emotionally fortified, and had a road map in hand, as it were. We started the day's journey with high spirits. Our goal lay a mere fifteen-kilometer trek away. Armed with the address of a contact person given to Gerhard by Czech parish members, we could count on finding shelter for the night and guidance on where best to cross the border into Hungary.

It was late afternoon when we reached the town indicated in the address, and soon thereafter we knocked at the specified street door. An elderly, refined-looking couple welcomed us warmly and with great politeness, notwithstanding our disheveled appearance. They had received word about us from our Czech friends—their relatives in Vršac—and were thus alerted to the possibility of our arrival.

The wife invited us to take off our wet coats and shoes for drying, and before we finished doing so, she returned from another room with an armful of woolen socks.

"You must be cold," she said, offering us the socks. Then, the couple escorted us to their day room where we sat close to their tile wood stove, soaking up the heat. The conversation soon moved from a mere formal exchange to the subject of our imprisonment and flight, and to our imminent goal.

The gentleman advised us to cross the border into Hungary from a certain village one hundred eighty-five kilometers to the north. The following morning we were to board a train that would get us to that village, and we would then cross the border into Hungary that very night. He would pay our train fare and refer us to a farmer in that village who, he was certain, would be able and willing to find an underground guide to show us to the border. Stunned by his foresight and generosity, we felt as if our journey were now moving fast and smoothly.

After a warm supper the lady had cooked for us, our host directed the conversation to faith. The dishes had been cleared and we still remained at the table.

The gentleman expressed his faith that "God's children stood under the heavenly Father's guidance and protection." To illustrate his point, he referred to a few Biblical examples, as well as examples from his own life. As if to reinforce our faith with concrete evidence, he suggested that he read our palms.

This startled me: faith, i.e., religion and palm reading? Our father would certainly have rejected outright the placing of faith in palm reading as hocus pocus, not to mention suspect on religious grounds. Our mother, on the other hand, who was by birth Catholic and in general less worried about such things, would probably have been less strict. However, neither Irmgard nor Gerhard refused to have their palms read. Thus, when my turn came—I happened to be the last, as I had been sitting at the end of the table—I quite eagerly, though still shyly, offered my hand. All our life lines, despite uneven shifting paths—yes, even breaks—persisted in growing wider and deeper, proving that we would prevail; reaching a ripe old age in which children were not absent.

"See, little one, you'll make it, and you'll have a good, long life; you will marry and have children," he concluded with a smile. Putting his arm around my hips, he drew me close to his side and held me firmly even when I strained to return to my seat.

Reading my distress at not feeling comfortable while also not wishing to imply any offense to our so generous host, Irmgard came to my aid:

"Come, Dorchen, let me, too, see what your lifeline is promising you."

I do not remember if, in the weeks following our palm readings, I actually had harkened back to seek reassurance in his words—but Puka is likely to have alluded to them with a joke when our luck was down. It wasn't until later years that I came to understand and appreciate the thoughtfulness of our host, who wished to send us on our danger-wrought journey with the gift of hope; for hope was the scaffolding of our inner house.

On retiring to the room provided for the night, we nevertheless began to feel overcome with the fear and dread of our upcoming border crossing. With only two nights passed since we crossed into Romania, our composure was frail. It was then that Gerhard first pulled out of his inner coat pocket the small Bible which he had brought from our parental home, and read a passage. This reading was followed by a prayer, in which he commended us and our undertaking to God's care. Irmgard notes that following this brief devotional, our fears were calmed as we lay down for the night.

Early the following morning, we boarded the train to the Hungarian border village. On entering a compartment, we broke into groups. Feeling some trepidation about not speaking Romanian, we had decided to studiously avoid being drawn into conversation with these outgoing and loquacious natives. We pretended to be dozing or looked through the windows intently.

It was noontime when the train pulled into the station. Getting off the train, still in groups, Irmgard and I at once spotted several *Vama* (local Romanian militiamen) who were looking for suspicious strangers; this being a border village. We passed them, assuming a carefree air—even laughing.

I clearly recollect that it was a brilliant, sunny winter day. Irmgard and I were walking down a wide street, which matched the address we had been given, looking for the farmer's house number. Puka was some distance behind us, and Gerhard and Hedy were even further back. We were only one or two houses away; we could already make out its broad, tall, whitewashed front, when two *Vamas* appeared from around the street corner. They were coming in our direction. We made every effort not to appear panic-stricken, although, of course, we were. We even continued to speak in German, knowing, as we did, that this village included a large number of ethnic Germans. The *Vama* passed without an incident.

A few more steps and we were at the street door. The door handle gave way, and we stepped into the courtyard. Trembling, we stood behind the closed door listening for steps while waiting for our heartbeats to slow down, and to regain our composure. A servant working in the kitchen spotted us and led us into a large room. We were face-to-face with an older, robust-looking farmer, who was sitting at the table with his wife having a midday dinner. Surprised by the appearance of two refugees who had been referred to his house on his acquaintance's recommendation, he was even more taken aback to learn that we had come for his assistance in arranging an underground guide.

He looked disgruntled. His ruddy cheeks, set off by a halo of white hair and his bright blue eyes, became flushed. His petite wife, appearing many years his junior, had deftly gone to the kitchen and returned with several plates. She quietly covered the dishes of food to keep them from getting cold. Although silent, her occasional glances were not unfriendly. Irmgard and I were still standing in our coats, some distance from the table. Even though Irmgard was the one who spoke, I also couldn't escape feeling the pain of humiliation, as I realized that our presence and appeal entailed discomfort and risks for this couple.

It felt so homelike: the large, yellow tile stove reaching toward the high ceiling, exuding warmth; the thick, uneven walls with the two inset bed spaces that held the plump mattresses filled with dry corn husks;

the enormous feather quilts and large, square feather pillows, both in home-spun linen cases; the beds high off the floor with two step stools by their sides. What a smile would come to one's face! What contentment one would feel lying back on those pillows, giving way to rest under those clouds of feathers! There would be no more dread of cold winter nights; tears and weariness would be taken away...

My imagining was interrupted. The farmer was clearing his throat: Okay, he would go and speak to a certain man who, he thought, would be willing to guide us to the Hungarian border. And we should do it tonight. Until then, we could stay at his place.

"Your acquaintance has done favors for me, so I will go right away to speak to a man who might be able to do that; he knows his way around in this area. It would be best if you went right away tonight. And in the meantime you can hide here somewhere, in the attic or hayloft."

Irmgard thanked him and reminded him rather apologetically that there were three more of us out on the street—which elicited a resigned and not too pleased, "Ach so? Na ja..."—*Oh really? Oh well..."*

He lifted himself up from his chair with his hands on the table. Standing tall and broad and slightly hunched over, he walked somewhat stiffly to the door. Turning, he said: "So, go and fetch your sister and brothers.

Hopefully I'll be back soon with an answer." His wife glanced at us, nodding as if she, too, were relieved.

As we returned to the courtyard, we saw him disappear through a door in the back of the farmyard. This suggested that the man the farmer was seeking out was a nearby neighbor, and that by going through his and the neighbor's back vegetable gardens and farmyards, he was going through the back door, so to speak. Irmgard sighed:

"Glad we got that behind us. It wasn't easy. In the end, he's doing it for the acquaintance who sent us. But in any event, he's helping us."

"He's probably afraid that word would get out, and then—" I suggested.

"Of course," said Irmgard. "And that would have bad consequences for him."

Out on the street, we saw Puka on the opposite side. As harbingers of good news, we smiled and waved to him. He, on the other hand, barely lifted his arm. As he crossed the street and came closer, we at once knew that something had happened. Pale, with fear in his eyes and his shoulders hunched as if to protect himself from something being hurled from behind, he told us that Gerhard and Hedy had been stopped by two *Vamas* and taken to the police station two blocks away. The news struck. We stared at each other; this was more than just the dashing of our new prospects and hope. As on the night of our flight, we were once again faced with an excruciating situation: Gerhard and Hedy in the hands of the *Vama* with the likelihood of imprisonment, while we were still free to flee to Hungary.

"Was machen wir jetzt?"—*What are we going to do now?* Irmgard asked in a voice that reflected our own wrenching thoughts.

"What now?" Irmgard repeated as she looked from one to the other. "The farmer is out looking for an underground guide, and we're supposed to flee tonight. But how can we go without the two? Just take off, leaving them to their own fate? What do you think?"

"No, we can't leave without them," Puka and I agreed. "Let's stay together."

After a moment's silence, Irmgard continued, "That means, then, that we're going to the *Vama* station and giving ourselves up voluntarily." Conflicting emotions were written all over her face.

"Yes," we concurred with fear and relief.

The decision was made. The heart had won. None of us had touched on what the others knew: turning ourselves in to be together and share our siblings' fate could mean being returned to Yugoslavian authorities.

When Irmgard and I returned to the farmhouse, the farmer looked cheerful. Yes, the man he had spoken to was willing to guide us to the Hungarian border, he told us, obviously pleased with the success of his mission. His consternation and disappointment were, therefore, all the greater when Irmgard relayed the events leading to the decision to turn ourselves in to the *Vama*.

"*Nein!*"—*No!* he almost shouted. Instead of turning ourselves in voluntarily, we should think of protecting ourselves and flee this very night. Our sister and brother might yet find a way to join us sometime later. But we didn't heed his advice. For us, it was a question of loyalty and love. How could we forsake them? Irmgard thanked the farmer and his wife for their help. Frustrated at first, in the end they wished us good luck and hoped that things would turn out for us despite the *Vama*, and that we'd reach Vienna.

Upon entering the *Vama* office, the two officers behind a desk looked up at us with surprise. Hedy and Gerhard, sitting on a bench facing the officers, looked even more startled to see us unaccompanied by a *Vama* officer, smiling in their direction. Hearing that we were turning ourselves in because we didn't want to be separated from our sister and brother, the officers were speechless. While Hedy's face took on a bittersweet expression, Gerhard's face showed unmistakable disappointment and disapproval. For, as he whispered in frustration when we joined them on the bench, from the moment of their apprehension he'd been keeping his eyes and ears open, already plotting their escape. But what might have been possible for two was an impossibility for five. Clearly, by following our hearts we had thwarted his plan to escape and flee with Hedy across the border which, as he had already found out, was "merely a stone's throw away"—*nur ein Steinwurf weg*.

When at one point I solicitously reached for his hand and, addressing him by his nickname, pleaded: "Gehad, without you we wouldn't have been able to do anything," he retorted with a wry smile and a resigned shrug of his shoulders: "Oh well, we'll see now what's going to happen."

I took his words as a peace offering, even if not approval. Though endowed with a greater pragmatic and strategic instinct than his four siblings, our older brother would almost certainly have made the same choice in reverse.

Prior to our arrival the two officers had taken down Hedy's and Gerhard's names, nationality, place of origin, and reasons for their illegal sojourn—and then searched them. And lo and behold, when searching Gerhard, they came upon a small treasure trove. There, on the inner side seams of his coat lining, hung like a row of tarnished little earrings secured by means of copper wire hooks, were some twenty pre-turn-of-the-century Habsburg silver ducats. Unhooking them one by one, the officers placed them into a little box, which they locked up inside a cupboard. They'd be kept safe there, the officers explained, until Gerhard's and Hedy's fate as well as that of the silver ducats had been decided. That Gerhard felt galled on both accounts—for their capture and for the robbery—can be easily imagined.

In the meantime, we three newcomers were as unaware of the officers' find and confiscation of Gerhard's treasures as we had been unaware of his possession of them. In the course of the afternoon hours that we spent sitting on the bench, side by side, trying to read the officers' faces like oracles of our destiny, Hedy had whispered under her breath something about silver and ducats they had found on Gerhard.

Though stunned and puzzled, we made no stir about it. The revelation quickly receded from our attention, captive as we were to the much bigger issue at hand: Would the officers' deliberations—during which they said that there were a number of very "grave considerations"—lead them to the decision to set us free, allowing us to escape to Hungary (a possibility they held out to us), or to imprison us, or to extradite us to Yugoslavia?

As early winter dusk began to filter into the room, the officers signaled that their day's duties had come to a close. Their deliberations would be resumed the following day. A guard was summoned, who took us to an adjoining room with two barred windows facing the street, and a large bench in the middle of the otherwise empty room. The floor of unfinished wide wooden planks was clean. The early evening light coming through the bars still lit up the room.

The guard seemed to see it as his duty to familiarize us with the additional features of our surroundings. First, he demonstrated to us that the door facing the office was locked. Then he drew us near a door behind the bench. Holding open the door, he motioned toward the room. Craning our necks, we saw a small table with two chairs and a cot. I glimpsed a small radio, or maybe a telephone, on a little bedside table. We nodded. We understood: This was his room. He was on duty tonight, and he was the assigned guard. We heard the key turn in the lock.

Darkness now filled the room. There were no lights. The five of us sat on the bench, huddling close to each other for comfort and warmth. We also didn't want to be overheard by our guard. In low voices, we exchanged notes on the events of the day, as well as questions and opinions on our prospects. Though our spirits were somewhat dampened, we were hopeful. We'd had no food all day and were hungry.

There were no indications that the *Vama* intended to provide food for us. There were no cots on which to sleep; no blankets with which to cover ourselves. Our brothers decided to sleep on the floor, thinking that they would be comfortable stretching out. We sisters would spend the night sitting on the bench, leaning against each other. We started: A door opened and shut. The sounds of voices and steps approaching from the guards' room were followed by the unlocking of our door. Stepping into the half-lit room was a woman with a basket in her hand. From her attire, we recognized her to be a Danube Swabian farmer woman.

Greeting us with *"Guten Abend"*—*Good evening*, she explained that she had brought us some food, as she was sure we'd be hungry. Folding back the linens from the basket, she handed us each warm food wrapped in parchment paper. Placing it into our outreached hands, she murmured her regrets, and wishes for good luck. Acknowledging our hunger, we openly expressed our appreciation and thanks. The guard stood in the doorway, looking on. We nodded our thanks to him as well when the woman turned to leave.

Word had evidently gotten out about us. The following night, another ethnic German woman was let in by the guard. As there was no food forthcoming from our captors, these meals of mercy from empathetic strangers were our life sustenance. It is quite possible, of course, that these Romanian ethnic German farmers were obliged to render such services. In either case, the meals were delivered with grace and generosity of heart. It bespoke a considerably less brutal communist regime with ethnic extremities than that operating in neighboring Yugoslavia.

Irmgard records that we spent three days and nights at this place, waiting in suspense for the officers' decision concerning us. It was a situation of vacillating emotions between the hope they held out for us, versus the "apparent obstacles" that prevented a quick decision. During the long hours of waiting, Gerhard told us two stories: the story of the silver ducats, and that of the woolen fabric. After our first meal, it was Puka who queried Gerhard about the origin of the valuable ducats.

"How did you come by them?"

"That's a long story,"—*Das ist eine lange Geschichte,* Gerhard replied.

"Yes, tell us," we sisters now urged. Gerhard seated himself in the middle, with Puka and me on either side of him. All five of us huddled close. Gerhard began in a low voice. Organized and particular as he was, he would tell his account in the sequence of their occurrence: the story of the woolen cloth first, then that of the silver ducats.

"*Also,*"—*So,* not long after the family's second

internment and his placement with his kind overseer at the winery, Gerhard twice, in the cover of the night, broke into our former family home, which was still unoccupied at that time. All the neighboring houses in this formerly predominantly ethnic German sector of Vršac had, under the supervision of the government, been taken over by settlers from distant mountainous regions of the country, such as Montenegro. At the mention of *"eingebrochen"*—*broke into,* I exclaimed,

"You did? What if they had caught you?" My voice betrayed both fear and qualm.

Puka, on the other hand, responded with a short, low whistle that signaled his admiration of his brother's daring, as well as his anticipation of a suspenseful story.

"Na, eingebrochen. . . ins eigene Haus!"—**Well, 'broke in'. . . into your own home!** Hedy mused.

"I did it in the hope of still finding something of value that would be helpful to us; to Mama and the youngest two," Gerhard explained, "such as those hundred dinar bills Mama had hidden and of course, her jewelry that Father and I buried in the cellar inside a jar not long before our first internment."

"And, did you find the jewelry and the money? Or was everything already gone?" Irmgard wondered.

"Come, let me tell things as they happened or you won't get to hear the story," admonished Gerhard, cutting short all questions until the end.

When allowed to visit our mother in the central internment camp in Vršac, Gerhard had learned from her about the hundred dinar bills hidden under the shelf lining in the armoire for linens. Based on several strolls he had taken after dark along the streets by our house, he decided that sometime close to midnight would be a safe time for his undertaking. The streets were empty and the houses dark, suggesting that the inhabitants were asleep. That the street lamp on the corner of our house was burned out, as were most of the street lamps up and down the two intersecting streets, was a godsend.

As we guessed, Gerhard chose to enter the house through one of the four windows on the side street lined with old acacia and chestnut trees. Given his acquaintance with the workings of the old window hardware, he had little trouble forcing open the window in our former "girls' room." Nor was it too difficult for him to find his way in the dark through the now mostly empty rooms, to the two large armoires in our parents' bedroom. Too large for easy removal by looters, they still stood in their former place.

Did he find the dinars? No. The looters who had been free to plunder all the thousands of former ethnic German-owned houses had taken not only all bed-, bath- and table-linens, suits, coats, and dresses stored in these armoires, but also the linen shelf-linings with

Mother's wide, handmade lace. Some lucky looter had also come upon the smoothly-pressed hundred dinar bills, stashed underneath for safekeeping as a little resource for the direst of needs.

"It must have been a woman," interjected Gerhard teasingly, "who couldn't resist the garlands with the angels—or was it cupids?"

"Roses in Mama's armoires, and angels in the armoires in the girls' room," corrected Hedy knowingly.

Returning to his story, Gerhard told how he had come upon the woolen cloth in the back of the bottom drawer in one of the two armoires, and how it seemed almost strange and miraculous to come across something in the rooms that felt like silent empty shells. He figured that the fabric had been either overlooked by the looters or its value underestimated; and how, though disappointed to find the money gone, he nonetheless climbed out of the house that night with a sense of satisfaction. Hidden under his coat, he held it pressed against his body. Thick and soft and many meters long, it served him first as a doubled-up warm blanket.

"Not too different from its intended purpose," he mused with a little laugh. He guessed that Mother had intended it for winter coats for two of her four older daughters, or that she had saved it for better or worse times. Hedy confirmed his guess, adding;

"It was a fawn-brown tweed, wasn't it?"

"Yes, and in the end it served all five of us, for it went toward the partial payment of our two underground guides."

Gerhard had come to the end of the story about the woolen cloth.

Intrigued, I expressed my thoughts aloud: "So, if Mama hadn't saved the fabric, but instead had Frau Kirschner or Herr Duček sew the coats for Hilda and Eri or for Hedy and Igat, then you couldn't have paid the guides with it and we wouldn't have been able to flee. Or would they have done it anyway?" At this, Irmgard, sitting next to me, put her arm around my shoulder. I knew she was smiling.

Returning on another night to our former home, Gerhard entered it as he had the first time. Picking up a small shovel in the storeroom at the staircase to the attic, he headed to the cellar. This time he had come armed with a flashlight, which he used circumspectly to avoid light escaping into the street from beneath the front door and through the cellar windows. Lifting the heavy metal door that was flush with the courtyard floor, he carefully laid it back; heedful not to make any noise.

He began to descend the steep staircase, passing the upper, small cellar level with a brick-laid floor where milk and yogurt were stored in the summer in brown ceramic jugs and jars, and blocks of sweet butter were floating in bowls with cold water. From there, he descended into the darker and mustier region that made us shudder as children at the ever-present possibility of a murderer hiding in the shadow of a corner, or underneath the staircase, or behind a damp wall; or of a snake slithering across the dirt ground to disappear under a pile of lumber; or a huge rat or mouse scurrying with beady eyes toward an unseen hole in the expanse of the cellar's darkness.

Gerhard knew where to look for the glass jar with our mother's jewelry. He had assisted our father in burying it soon after the Russian military invasion and the pilferage of watches, sliver, and jewelry began. There, where the staircase ended and a dim patch of daylight cast through the cellar windows, he observed the raised mound of good earth in which carrots, parsnips, and potatoes once lay buried under a light cover to last through the harsh winter months until the time of new crops.

But the jar wasn't there.

Hooding his flashlight with his jacket, Gerhard began to dig along the head of the mound, then inside. He proceeded to dig in a fanned out radius. On his third or fourth attempt his shovel hit on an object. Kneeling down, he used his hands to clear away the dirt. He lifted out a glass jar about the height of his palm. His flashlight revealed that the contents were not golden, but grey in color. So it wasn't our mother's jewelry. Yet he was certain that they were of value. Why else had the jar been buried, but for safekeeping?

Thrusting the jar into his coat pocket, he quickly covered up all the holes and left the cellar, laying the metal door quietly back over its entrance. On his way through the house he went by our father's study, opened the bookcase, and took out a soft, leather-bound, pocketbook-size Bible, which he put in his other pocket. It was the Bible he carried with him on our flight and from which he would read to us with increasing frequency over time.

The bottle Gerhard had come upon in his search for Mother's jewelry contained some twenty rare silver ducats from the early days of the Habsburg emperor Franz Josef's reign. They were of considerable value. Whose were they, and who had buried them in our cellar? My three older siblings were quite certain that they weren't our parents', for they had never seen nor heard of them, nor had our mother mentioned them when she spoke to Gerhard of the hidden dinars and jewelry.

My siblings concluded that they must have belonged to the elderly neighbor couple, the Meiers, who had come to live with us soon after the Russian occupation. Hedy now vaguely recalled seeing Frau Meier one afternoon, carrying something in her hand when she and Mother entered Father's study—and seeing, not long thereafter, Father crossing the courtyard and turning the corner that led to the cellar, with a small shovel in his hand.

"And you kept them?" I wondered uneasily.

"Should I have buried them again to leave for eternity? Or should I have taken them to the police to hand them over to the Yugoslav government so that they could confiscate them in addition to everything they already took from all of us? The silver ducats would never have gotten back in the hands of the Meiers since they probably didn't even survive the first few months of their internment. Who knows where they had been placed? Probably in a camp to die. I figured that they were a final gift that would be put to good use; that they would see us through our flight—and, as I had hoped, Mama's too—and would help us with a start in Vienna."

"And now they're all gone," noted Puka wistfully.

"Not quite all," Gerhard quietly said.

"No?" Puka and I exclaimed. But Gerhard didn't answer; we knew by now that he considered it prudent to not divulge what could, under certain circumstances, work against us.

Quietly, I pondered how one can look for a treasure and not find it, and instead find another that you didn't look for or expect. When asked what I thought of the story, I responded:

"Oh, I'm thinking of Frau Meier's angel eyes which Herr Meier loved and admired so."

Alluding to Frau Meier's "angel eyes" evoked a certain lightness as well as recollections of this gentle, white-haired couple that had lived in the stately corner house across from us. Until the end of World War I, Herr Meier had served as an officer in the army of the Habsburg Austro-Hungarian Empire. Thereafter, he held a bookkeeper position in the City Hall of Vršac. They had one daughter who, after finishing her training at the local school of pedagogy, left for a teaching position in Belgrade, moving back home to be with her elderly parents only shortly before the Russian invasion. From a few conversations Irmgard had with the daughter, Irmgard surmised that the parents' absorption with each other made the daughter feel superfluous, if not in their way— as though nothing appeared able to displace the bliss they experienced in each other.

Shortly after the communist takeover, the Meiers' house was confiscated for Russian officer quarters. Told to move in with their neighbors across the street, they approached our parents. And although there had been only a courteous neighborly relationship between the two families, our parents took them in and gave them their own beautiful, large bedroom to live in. Amongst the few treasures the Meiers brought with them was a box of their cards from their courtship days. Following our family's brief respite at home after our first internment, one or two of my siblings and I had come upon this box. In one of these romantic picture postcards from pre-World War I days that depicted little winged angel heads in the four corners, the then young, and doubtless, strapping, smart-looking Officer Meier—stationed perhaps in Budapest or near Vienna—likened his beloved's "incomparably" beautiful eyes to angel eyes.

Though we were, admittedly, not yet romantically inclined, this struck us as an example of perfect love and exemplified the errant, and thus suspect, judgment of one in love. For, where his loving eye saw sublime beauty, the uninspired, ordinary eye saw imperfection. Frau Meier's eyes were then, as now, of two different colors: one a bright light blue, the other a deep hazel.

In the afternoon of our second day at the *Vama*, we were summoned to the room of the two officers. Though hopeful, we couldn't help feeling some trepidation. Would they let us cross into Hungary, as they had repeatedly assured us after hearing our story? Or would they extradite us to Yugoslavia, as they had indicated initially?

Sitting behind their desks, the two officers appeared rather distant. With the help of the translator, they began reviewing the protocol. All the facts they had written down were based solely on our words, since we had no form of proof of either our birth or nationality.

That we didn't have a permit or passport was, of course, evidence of our illegal entrance into Romania.

The officers expressed their regret. Because they didn't have the authority to decide our case, they were forced to send us on to a higher command some fifty kilometers away, who had the power to do so. Clearing his throat, the officer conducting the interview turned to the issue of the silver coins. He looked at Gerhard who, like the rest of us, had been silently listening and waiting for their communiqué. Though pale and visibly affected by the news, he looked the officer in the eye. The officer then turned to Irmgard. She, too, returned his gaze and remained silent.

The two *Vama* officers glanced at each other, whereupon the second officer took from a locked cupboard a small wooden box. Standing a few feet from the desk, we glimpsed a little pile of old tarnished coins with little holes in the center and brass hooks attached to them. There was a suspenseful silence. Clearing his throat again, the officer now declared in a noticeably clipped voice that Gerhard must sign a statement saying that he was turning all the silver ducats over to the Romanian state as their rightful owner. When Gerhard's signature was in place, and we turned to leave, the officer tried to reassure us once more:

"Don't worry, they will let you go to Hungary."

Back in our room, Gerhard, who had been pacing back and forth, paused by the windows before joining us on the bench. Shock and apprehension had kept us silent. Now first one, then the other began to give utterance to them. When Gerhard finally spoke, his voice seemed almost light:

"We might yet see and seize a chance to escape into Hungary, either on our way to the place they are taking us to or from that place itself."

"Wie denn?"—*How*? The guards will have guns," I moaned with a plaintive voice. Irmgard drew me to her.

"Dorchen, you're trembling all over!" Her voice was soft and pitying.

Sighing deeply, Gerhard suggested: *"Beten wir!"*—*Let's pray*. He began: "I shall lift my eyes to the hills from whence shall cometh my help..." And we felt calmer.

Daylight had almost faded when the door was opened and, as on the night before, our warden and a local peasant woman, bundled up in a large woolen winter shawl, stood in the doorway. Pointing modestly to the basket on her arm, she explained that she had brought some food. She handed us each some home-baked peasant bread, a generous slice of smoked ham, a piece of freshly-baked yeast cake, and an apple. Hungry, incredulous and thankful, we told her that it felt like Christmas. She smiled, pleased. Taking in the unheated, cold room, she expressed her hope that the food might make us feel a little warmer on the inside and that we might sleep better. We assured her it would.

Irmgard refers to our nights as wretchedly cold, and our sleep as fitful and nightmarish. With no covers other than the clothes on our bodies, and all of us by now bundled together lying on the bare wooden floors at freezing temperatures, we had difficulty falling asleep and staying asleep. Trembling, with chattering teeth, we pressed against each other to both share and preserve our body heat. Barely fallen asleep, we'd re-awaken from freezing cold, or start from our own or someone else's nightmares. Calm and rest came only in the early hours.

We had spent most of the third day at the *Vama* without speaking; each to himself, our spirits weighed down as by a heavy gray blanket. Dusk hadn't yet set in, when Irmgard suddenly broke the silence: "Gerhard, I think I figured it out."

All four of us looked at her. "They expected that we'd offer the silver coins to them. They would have allowed us to cross the border into Hungary, if we had bribed them. The idea of bribing them didn't even occur to us!"

"You probably are right." Gerhard nodded slowly, an ironic smile playing around his lips. "Hence suddenly the lack of authority."

Clearing his throat, Puka, alluding to the *Vama*

officer's disingenuous words, quipped: "Don't worry, you'll get to go to Hungary," succeeding in making us laugh despite our dejection. He had introduced a motif that he would henceforth use unexpectedly with appropriate variations at crucial moments, causing us to laugh even in the face of bitterly shattered hope, highlighting for a moment not only disingenuous promises, but also the irony in our childlike trust and hope—seemingly proven an illusion.

4

THROUGH A FOREST OF BIRCH TREES

Luckily, each of us had saved our apples; either for the following day or for the forthcoming journey. There was no food to come on the third evening, or on the morning of our departure when we set out on our march in the company of two *Vama* soldiers with guns over their shoulders. If we started out with the lingering hope while still a mere stone's-throw from the Hungarian border, their guns and the impact of what was about to unfold before our eyes and inside each of us, would soon dispel escape as an option.

Irmgard's account comments that the two guards, though indifferent to us, were not unkind. Once outside the village, we were urged to quicken our pace. We turned onto a path along a river that was wet and slippery. Gray fog enveloped the landscape. Eventually, we entered a forest of birch trees where the silence was so deep, it felt ominous. Were they going to shoot us here where no one could hear it? We walked through this forest of white and gray-mottled tree trunks as condemned men might walk to their execution. Hedy reached for my hand and I dug my nails into hers. I can still see my brothers' ashen, suspenseful faces as they staggered a few yards ahead. The two would break into gallows humor, while we sisters walked behind in silence.

Coming out of the forest, we saw a river that looked as gray as the sky. Pointing to it, the guards excitedly repeated, *"Marosch! Marosch!"*

Irmgard and Gerhard acknowledged recognition—he from his geography lessons, she also from stories and songs she remembered for their sad and dark mood. As with the Moldau in Czechoslovakia, many a tragic fable and story was staged at its banks and in its waters. Seeing its gray, leaden movement, she understood why.

A shadowy object in the distance was moving toward the bank that we were approaching. It was a barge that had come to ferry us across. We embarked with trepidation, and remained apprehensive as it glided silently over the still, dark waters to the river's other shore.

Capturing the anguishing experience on that morning, Irmgard, in her account, admits to a torturous sense of uncertainty and fear about our destination and fate. The whistling, joking and laughter between our two guards touched her as callous; like a sneering, musical accompaniment to our misery. Entering the dense forest where every sound is muted and absorbed and not a soul would be seen for the density of the trees, the thought that this might be the chosen place for our execution suggested itself powerfully to her imagination, as it did to mine. Subsequently, pushing off the shore and reaching deeper waters, she couldn't rid herself of the feeling that the barge was moving us toward a place of no return. Finally, glancing over the edge into the impenetrable, dark water, she for a moment felt herself drawn to leap in and find an end from our unabated misery.

The barge had reached the other shore. Disembarking, we glanced at each other with inaudible sighs of relief; anguish still written on our faces. We had made it through the forest and across the river, but what was awaiting us? The fear that we would be deported back to Yugoslavia hung over us.

We were approaching a village. Vigilantly, Irmgard and Gerhard were looking for strategic points of reference that would prove helpful in the event that there might yet be a chance of escape. They surmised that the Hungarian border was also only five kilometers from this village, and that it lay to the northwest. This was welcome news that helped lift our spirits.

It was shortly after noon when we arrived at the Vama station. As we sat on a bench in front of a building in a compound, curious soldiers and Vama officers soon gathered in front of us, staring inquisitively and asking questions. Not knowing the language, we sat there mute; our head covers close to our faces, and our coat collars turned up. This quickly elicited jokes and laughter. Yet, when our officer guards told them something about us, their response shifted. Trying to boost our spirits and comfort us, the soldiers and officers eagerly reassured us that we'd be sent to Hungary. The Romanians were compassionate people, they told us.

Several rushed off, then returned with food they had gotten from their provisions; others offered us their cots and beddings for some rest and sleep, which we accepted with incredulous smiles and sincere thanks.

Later, after dusk, two new guards fetched us to take us to our night quarters. It was raining. Walking among dismal surroundings, we walked into a vast courtyard with slippery mud and large potholes of water. Careful not to slip and fall, we slowly approached a long, white building with a wide-open door. Billowing clouds of light and steam filled its frame. Soon the stench, more acrid and intense than any of us had ever encountered, told us that we were approaching a stable.

It was a vast garrison stable, buzzing with high energy and sounds. Through steaming vapors as through moving veils, we beheld the enormous brown and black bodies of horses: pawing, neighing; with craned necks and tossing manes, their fiery eyes turned to the unlit hidden cavern of the stable where soldiers in shirts and with their caps to one side emerged with large forks of hay that they pitched into the racks in front of the horses. Laughing, whistling, yelling to each other and the horses, the soldiers filled the stable with a clamor of loud, merry sounds.

We stood and looked, stunned. We were to sleep here? Already, soldiers were dropping forks of straw on the ground some three feet from the hind legs of the horses. With gestures and motioning, our guards and the soldiers made us understand that this was our bedstead for the night. Gerhard and Irmgard pointed to the horses' hind legs, as we would clearly be within the range of their possible kicks. The men tried to reassure us and dispel our concern. Perhaps seeing Gerhards's skeptical smile and raised eyebrows, and Irmgard's unmistakably unhappy look, the guards instructed the soldiers to move our straw bedding a foot or two further from the horses.

Nodding our thanks, we let ourselves down on the straw. When the guards left and the doors closed behind them, Puka, glancing up with his deep-set eyes from the damp straw underneath the horses to the vapor clouds above, observed:

"Well, at least we won't be freezing here."

"Yes, and in the meantime we're also able to breathe," retorted Irmgard with a nasal voice that expressed how offensive the stable stench was to her senses, as she held her nose shut with her fingers.

Settling down onto the straw for the night, Gerhard entreated us sisters to keep our eyes shut and pretend to be asleep, no matter what—to respond to no one. But falling asleep or even pretending to be asleep was not easy. Soldiers tending to horses walked past our heads, heedless of the straw that was dropping onto our faces. Though toned down from at first, the stable remained alive with voices, whistles and laughter. From time to time a number of soldiers would congregate at our feet and look at us and make comments. At one point we heard one call a comrade who, after exchanging some words with him in Romanian, announced:

"*Nachad, wie schen!*"—*My, how beautiful,* and with slight variation again, "*Nachad, so schen!*"—*My, so beautiful.* This little phrase prefixed with the Hungarian exclamatory would become Puka's second refrain through our journey.

When the voices and activities finally subsided and the lights were turned low, Irmgard whispered, half outraged, half aghast: "Something is biting me, I'm sure it's lice."

"It's the straw that's pricking you," Gerhard

whispered back, assuaging. Shortly, Irmgard protested anew: She was certain she was being bitten by lice, for the bites she felt were where no straw was touching her.

"I'm not feeling anything," Puka volunteered cheerfully. By now, Hedy and I were beginning to scratch ourselves—now here, now there, declaring unhappily that we, too, were being bitten.

"Perhaps it's only fleas," our brother Gerhard whispered encouragingly.

"Only!" we three sisters objected in unison.

I woke up with a start. The light had been turned on, lighting up the length of the stable. The others began to move too. So, we had slept deeply after the first fitful hours. Hedy looked wide awake, as if she had been awake for some time. She returned my sideways glance with a resigned smile, her eyes not smiling.

Suddenly, the two-part door was thrown open from the outside. A wave of freezing cold air rushed in, unfurling over our faces. Shivering, we nonetheless breathed it in like morning balm. Outside was early dawn; the coming day still wresting itself from the embrace of the waning night.

Behind our heads, the rustling, stamping and scraping sounds of the risen horses, neighing up and down the scale as if tuning and testing their vocal chords for the coming day, intermingled with buzzing shouts and whistles. The day's business had begun: new fodder being distributed, pungent dripping straw raked up, piles of fresh straw brought in for replacement.

It was time for us to rise. Hedy had to first turn over to her side and support herself on her arms to get up. We pulled up our socks and stockings, brushed down our coats, removed our head covers and shook them out, and brushed over our hair to remove clinging straw and straighten its disheveled look. We girls folded our scarves and tucked them into our coat pockets, while the boys placed their caps back on their heads, over one eye and slightly down, guided by old habit.

"Fesch"—Smart, Hedy said, drawing out the word teasingly. Irmgard spied through the open stable door a well and trough into which a steady stream of clear water was flowing through a narrow pipe. Apart from some low-roofed, mud-splashed white buildings off to the sides – perhaps barracks or hay lofts – well and trough were the only thing in the large yard; that looked like an empty, barren field studded with holes filled with frozen water from last night's rain.

"Maybe they'll allow us to wash ourselves in the trough," Irmgard called out with a perked-up voice and face.

"Making a better impression on the authorities would probably not hurt. Perhaps they'll even let us run off to Hungary," joked Gerhard.

"Imagine, Igat, you'll also be able to brush your teeth," Puka added with a grin.

"I hope you all intend to clean yours," came back Irmgard.

"Of course, even if in our case the effect won't be the same" Puka retorted.

"Pardon me!" Gerhard now interjected, pretending to take offense. Both he and Irmgard knew that they had perfect teeth. Irmgard tended to hers conscientiously.

Our guards stood in the doorway, dressed in uniforms, guns over their shoulders. As with Gerhard's mention of "authorities," so the sight of the guards now sent a tremor through us: today the verdict. What is it going to be? Again, our faces took on a solemn look.

Yes, we were free to wash ourselves in the trough. The guards stood back as we washed our faces in the clear, bluish, icy water. Pulling out her toothbrush from her coat pocket, Irmgard brushed her teeth with the clear water, while the rest of us (who had lost our brushes long ago along the way) rubbed them with a finger. Then, using the boys and Hedy as a screen, Irmgard and I quickly unbraided our hair, hers dark and mine a light brown. Brushing through it with our fingers, we quickly braided our hair again and stepped forward.

Beyond this early morning scene in the crisp air at the trough, preening ourselves for our interview with the "sufficiently-empowered authorities," my memory of the subsequent early developments of that day is a blank page. Neither the momentum of storytelling, nor the facts noted in Irmgard's account are able to recapture the vanished imprints of what followed in the ensuing hours. Perhaps what followed the hopeful beginning turned out so shattering that a certain protective mechanism quickly swallowed or erased them.

Gathering from Irmgard's account, the hope that the new morning had held for us was soon dashed with the information that the decision on our case rested with the central commando of the *Vama* located in the city of Arad, a town about twenty miles due east.

When we arrived there, we were first placed into a small, evil-smelling cell furnished with nothing but a tiny, open, barred window on the upper end of a wall. A filthy cement floor revealed the source of the cell's retching smell. The young inmate locked up in it for several days already informed us that it was also infested with lice. We didn't know how long we would be held here. Horror was staring into our face.

In an hour's time, a sergeant came to take us to the central commando. Lined up before the appointed officials, we stood a long time waiting. As Irmgard notes in her account, the three elegantly-dressed gentlemen were in no hurry. The interrogation commenced; they showed little interest in our case. Untouched throughout by any sense of urgency, we were discharged, a decision still pending.

The sergeant, who struck Irmgard as considerably more sympathetic than the gentlemen, returned us not to the terrifying little cell but to a garrison stable. It seems that we now embraced our new quarters as a certain boon, notwithstanding its stable odor and the two horses that occupied intermittently one third of its space; the darker back part of it. It was warm here and there were unused hay racks and hay boxes into which we could crawl for warmth and sleep; the boys in the racks, Irmgard and I in the boxes. In consideration of her painful back, Hedy would sleep on the cot near the stable door. The stable smell, considerably less pungent than in the other stable the night before, no longer fazed us much.

This stable that sheltered us within its four thick walls, and became stage and backdrop of many a story and scene unrolling within its space and reach, stands before my mind's eye like a humpbacked, lowly, little fort. Though without windows, its two-section door of thick, weather-beaten wood, closed at night from the inside for warmth and barred for safety, could be opened up in the daytime for fresh air, light, and a piece of gray or blue sky.

Irmgard found herself the following morning assigned the job of an aid to the garrison cook. In her free morning hours, she and the rest of us were charged with the daily cleaning of garrison offices and rooms. We wouldn't have minded the work, as it meant change of scenery, more light and better air; but—as Irmgard notes—"...for the constant jokes and mockery to which we sisters were subjected by the soldiers. The combination of being women, prisoners, and not speaking and understanding their language made us defenseless targets."

Emerging from the stable door we could be seen walking in the morning past an old, malfunctioning water pump and a half-filled trough, following a diagonal path past a little house this side of the long, covered entrance drive, to the buildings with even rows of windows on the other side of that drive. Past noon, we'd be seen retracing this path in reverse direction. We had left hungry in the morning and we returned hungrier yet at noon. The amount and substance of food portioned out to us in the evening could not abate our hunger. Irmgard's path in the afternoon stopped at the little building this side of the covered garrison entrance. At night a guard with a gun over his shoulder stood guard at this portal.

Shortly, I too was assigned to work as an aid to the garrison cook. Irmgard and I were glad to work together. Our job consisted of assisting the cook with the preparation of hefty and, for the most part, one-dish dinners, followed by after-dinner cleanup of dishes and pots. Our duties lasted from early afternoon to late evening hours. We had hoped that this working assignment in the kitchen would bring us some extra food that we could share with our famished brothers. But the cook proved to be miserly, and the little we could spare from our own none-too-generous portions was too little to abate their growing hunger. The cook's callousness surprised us, as he was half-ethnic German himself, knew our story, and was quite affable in general; even if also often grumpy. His grumpiness we attributed to his advanced years and arthritis, as well as to the hardships of his job. There seemed a flow of communication between the garrison commander and him.

Located in a compact two-room building, the small kitchen was adjoined by a yet-smaller room with an opening and a partial wall between them. Through the open space in the wall between the two rooms, one could see a narrow cot against the far wall and a wooden table against the partial wall. In the right front corner of the room one door opened to the kitchen, the other to the outside; the garrison courtyard.

Then two more prisoners joined us in the stable. In consideration of its limited space, a new sleeping plan was devised. Our brothers would give up the hay racks to the newcomers and move to the hay boxes. Hedy would continue to sleep on the cot in the stable, while Irmgard and I would sleep on the table in the room next to the kitchen. What at first may have seemed an enviable solution turned out rather torturous and disconcerting, for not only did the table top prove much too narrow for two, and unyieldingly hard—but to our dismay, we discovered the cook to be sleeping in the room with us, on the cot. We didn't protest. You feared to oppose and in any way offend those in whose hands your fate lay. In this case, it appeared to have been the garrison commandant's instructions.

5

UNLUCKY BIRDS

The two male prisoners instantly call up the image of scarecrow; *"Vogelscheuchen"* in German. Skinny; their narrow black pants end somewhere below the calf and ankle, exposing bare, matchstick legs. The companion jackets cut for fourteen-year-olds, reach barely beyond their waists, the sleeves inches above their wrists make the bony forearms and hands appear peculiarly awkward. The lapels of the tight buttoned-up jackets, held together with large safety pins, gape at the shoulders, revealing scrawny bird-like necks, craning from snug, collarless shirts, brown from months of dust and sweat. Strings hold dirt-caked soles and shoes together and secure them to the feet. The confirmation suits of fourteen-year-old boys turned into a masquerade.

The older one is the shorter and quieter of the two. His eyes and hair color are of an indefinite dull brown. The younger, taller, and more talkative one has bright—though sparse—red-blond hair and pale blue eyes that shift about like a fowl's, only quicker. Blue veins protrude alarmingly from his temples and forehead.

They speak German. Their speech tells us that they are *"Reichsdeutsche,"* Germans from Germany proper, the "Reich." We guess that they were former German soldiers who served somewhere at the eastern front. Quietly, we wonder if they had defected from their warring ranks when defeat was palpable and visible everywhere, or if they were defectors from Russian prisoner-of-war camps. It being winter 1946, the latter seems more likely.

They appear glad to be with German speaking prisoners, even if we are not from the "Reich" and thus not quite authentic Germans, as well as being "mere kids." They soon confide in us as to ex-patriots. As we had guessed, they are defectors from Russian prisoner-of-war camps and had been taken captive at the eastern front. They had exchanged their military uniforms for the civilian clothes they were wearing, given to them by merciful farmers somewhere in Russia, or Poland. They have been on the run for seven months, traversing lands on foot, hiding often in daytime, trekking across fields, hills and mountains at night. Always skirting towns and villages, they sometimes stole into haylofts for cover or sleep. They've fed themselves on what they could find in the fields, orchards, and hills, slowly putting kilometer after kilometer behind them. And now here, so close to home, *"dieses Pech!"*—*this bad luck.*

In the daytime, they chose to sit in the hay racks, their legs and feet dangling down from between the rods, while we, in our free hours, were sitting on the cot; standing or walking back and forth, looking up at them and listening when one or the other was telling his stories. It wasn't difficult to make the younger one with the sparse red hair and scrawny long neck talk and tell their tales of frozen feet, encountered dangers, near-misses and varied hardships.

Puka, listening to their stories as to adventures, would goad the storytellers on. Gerhard's questions, directed usually to the older of the two, more often pertained to such specifics as battles, places, numbers, prison conditions, and the configurations of certain terrains. The older, quieter one with the duller hair and brown eyes inquired about our whereabouts and reasons for our detention. Perhaps he had left a young wife and small children behind when he was called up for duty at the front to "defend his Motherland," and knew not if they were alive or had perished.

Hedy soon would not turn and face them while listening to their stories as Puka, Gerhard and I did, though she was clearly listening, even if with a closed face. Had she grown tired of them? *"Wie Vögel"*—*Like birds* she once said, shrugging her shoulders. And they looked like birds in their scarecrow attire, perched on the racks. *"Und schau dir unseren Spassvogel an!"*—*And look at our joker,* she added with a nod toward Puka. Some time later, she continued this "Vogel" motif by referring to them with a wry smile as *"die Pechvögel"*— *the unlucky fellows,* adding after a bit, *"wir alle"*—*all of us.*

Did Hedy draw a line somewhere beyond which she withheld her empathy with the hardships and misfortune of these German soldiers, holding them responsible, as it were, for the calamity Nazi Germany had brought to millions—and in the process, also upon themselves? Perhaps she didn't forget that our fate, as indicting as it was to its perpetrators, in the end was the result of the vengeance brought on by Nazi Germany.

It's a holiday, perhaps a Romanian state holiday marking its "liberation" by the Russian Soviet army from fascist rule, and consequent establishment of Romania's communist government. The day commands a festive celebration. The cook is in a good mood. There will be a special meal for the soldiers in the garrison, and wine, plenty of wine. All the necessary ingredients have been delivered. The commandant has been generous. "Today we're going to cook a real dinner. Everyone is to be happy and celebrate. There will be more preparations, so we'll be starting early," the cook informs us jovially.

Our brothers hope that the cook might send them some leftovers.

Hours of hands in cold water; rinsing, washing, peeling and chopping. Burning chapped hands, aching backs and feet from standing long hours in the same place and position. Clouds of steam rising from huge pots, fogging up the windowpanes and walls and filling the small kitchen. The windows have come to look like slate boards that children learn to write the alphabet and numbers on. It's dark outside and soldiers begin to arrive. The taller ones have to duck their heads stepping through the low door frame, a posture some keep to avoid hitting the ceiling.

They are jovial; they laugh and speak with loud voices. Anticipating a holiday meal and wine, they feel generous and want everyone to be happy. They greet the cook's kitchen assistants; want us to share in the festivities. We're to have some wine too, which the cook eagerly pours for us. Cups get raised, toasts are made, and with each new crowd the cook, unusually generous, urges more wine on us. Unaccustomed to it, and with barely as much as a piece of bread in our stomachs on that day, we at once feel the wine's effect.

Our mother's image rises up in my memory. Two Russian sergeants, stationed in the corner house across from ours, knock one evening at our kitchen door, each with a watering can filled with red wine. They wish to celebrate our return home from our first brief internment. With Father and Gerhard still in a prison labor camp somewhere, Mother presides as family head and hostess. Sitting around the table the sergeants affably urge her and the "pretty daughters"—referring to Hedy and Irmgard, for Claudi and I still pass as mere girls—to toast and join in the drinking. Anxious not to displease or offend the self-invited, occupying military guests for fear of a certain unpredictable and volatile temperament, Mother and her daughters raise and take sips from their glasses. She is keeping the soldiers engaged in a continuous flow of conversation about their parents, siblings, Russian winters, their holiday customs, her personal regrets about the suffering visited on the Russian people at the hands of the German Wehrmacht. She is speaking in Serbian, they are answering in Russian with Irmgard as occasional linguistic mediator.

Despite the women's drawn-out sipping, their glasses do in time get empty. While they're being refilled with much bravado, Mother is looking at Puka and then at the metal wood bucket by the wood-burning stove where he is sitting. Observant and quick-minded as he is, he casually picks up the bucket and places it at Mother's side. Hours pass. Refilled glasses are raised to the lips, and by and by, inconspicuously emptied into the metal container. Following Mother's numerous gracious reassurances that no, she was not yet so tired that she needed to go to bed, leaving her two "pretty daughters" in charge of her guests, the drowsy, half-bewildered looking sergeants retreat shortly before midnight.

Irmgard and I keep raising the cups to our lips and keep pouring wine into the pail with vegetable cuttings.

Quiet has settled over the kitchen. Tired and stiff with arthritis, the cook dishes up plates full of food for himself and the two of us. With the larger portion left on our plates, Irmgard and I hurry with them across the dimly lit courtyard to the stable. With what eager eyes our brothers look at the food, how the three devour it, their hunger only teased, not sated by it. Irmgard and I return to the kitchen, the plates licked clean.

We're cleaning up, washing and drying mounds of dishes. The cook has two large caldrons of water boiling. He pours wine and presses the cups into our hands. He wants to hear no protests: we've worked hard, helped him, the wine's here, we deserve the reward. He notes that little Dori—if he may call her so as her sister does—is looking quite tired and sleepy. It's been long hours and we've been so good, and so we shall have a treat tonight: a bath. Wouldn't we like a nice, warm bath? Wouldn't that feel good? Oh yes, it would feel like heaven, we think to ourselves, but do not say it. Well, little, tired Dori, who looks like she's barely able to keep her eyes open, should stop drying dishes and take a bath. Look, there in the adjoining room behind the table stands the tub, all ready. We just pour some water into the tub, all ready and waiting on the stove, temper it with cold water, just right, and little Dori can have her bath while he and Irmgard finish up the kitchen work. And after her bath, little Dori can lie down on the cot and rest until Irmgard is done with her bath.

I, who for many weeks hadn't had warm water to wash my hands and face in, and couldn't remember when I last had a warm bath, found the warm water soothing, as soothing as a warm home and a Mother's arms. Putting my clothes back on again, I lay down on the cot where, feeling sleepy and soothed, I immediately fell asleep.

I open my eyes. It is dark in the room. I don't understand. I feel a hand on me. I awake with a bolt. I know it is the cook who is lying beside me. Thrusting his hand away, I call:

"Igat?"... There is no answer.

"Wo ist sie?"—*Where is she?* I ask. Lying on the outer side of the cot, I'm up with a leap, tear my coat away from his grip and run to the door.

"*Nein, bleib!*"—*No, stay!* He protests, as he is trying to get up from the cot. The door is locked and the key is not in the lock. Terrified, I feel the ground with my hand. Brush across the threshold. It isn't there. Desperately, I feel in the corner. O there — the key! It is a large, heavy old key, almost the length of my hand. With shaking fingers, I'm trying to find the keyhole. There. But my fingers tremble so, I can't get the key in—and his hobbling is coming closer and closer. And then, what a blessing,— the key is in. I turn the key as he grabs me by the arm. I pull open the door and run out, tearing my coat sleeve from his clasp.

"*Nein, komm zurück, bleib!*"—*No, come back, stay!* he calls.

A guard with a gun over his shoulder looks on. I'm running across the large, barely-lit courtyard toward the stable, calling:

"Gerhard! Gerhard!" The cook is following me, growling, "Come back!"

Oh, that Gerhard would hear me! What if he isn't hearing me through those thick walls and in his sleep? What if I can't slip into the stable in time and the cook catches up with me—? Then, like a miracle, the stable door opens and Gerhard stands in the doorway: a tall, upright figure as if lit against the dark. I'm running toward him; with a few quick steps he is by my side.

"*Er, er...*"—*He, he...*" I stammer with eyes torn

wide open. Gerhard is looking at the cook, who still wants me to return.

"*Is ja gar nix, sie tut nur so—*" *It's nothing, she's just acting like*—he insists.

"*Die Dora bleibt hier!*"—*Dora is staying here*, Gerhard declares decisively. Inside the stable, he slides the large wooden bar across the door. It's pitch dark. I hear rustling coming from the hay racks and the hay box. With his hand on my shoulder, Gerhard guides me to the cot.

"Come, lie down with Hedy and sleep! You're safe now."

"*Was ist passiert?*"—*What happened?* Hedy whispers.

"*Der Koch... Die Igat... ist die Igat hier?*"—*The cook... Igat... is Igat here?* I stutter, teeth and body chattering with fits of shivers.

"*Nein.*"—*No.*

"Pst!" Gerhard hushes us. I hear him settling into the hay box. There is more rustling as the other men turn or lie back. Before too long sleep envelops me, delivering me from the tremors of cold and shock.

The next morning, Irmgard arrives at the stable. She looks pale but collected. Noticing our anxious faces, she slowly shakes her head as if to reassure us that no ill has befallen her. Later, sitting on the cot beside me, she wonders:

"Were you here all night?" I shake my head.

"Where were you?" I asked her. "I woke up... and he

was... and the door was locked and the key gone... but I did get away just in time." Nodding and cupping my cheek with her firm, soft hand, she said,

"Poor, Dori!" adding after a moment with a deep sigh: "I, too, was lucky. I'll tell you sometime."

On Monday morning Irmgard and I were instructed to clean windows in the garrison offices. Standing on the windowsills, we had to stretch and stand on our toes in order to reach the upper panes. Soldiers made it their pastime to stand around, calling out things to each other, laughing and joking. Rumors had obviously gotten around. Gerhard, who was cleaning offices nearby, made a point of dropping in from time to time, exchanging a few words with us, thus trying to keep things in check. Irmgard's and my tasks as kitchen aides to the cook came to an abrupt end. We didn't show up at the kitchen on Sunday, nor were we ordered to return to it thereafter. Instead, we were assigned to clean offices in the mornings.

In the coming days I spent the afternoon hours lying on the cot with closed eyes or, if the stable door was open, looking out at the sunny or overcast gray sky. I felt as I had as a child after a siege of deliriously high temperature, such as when I had been ill with scarlet fever. I was in shock. I, too, no longer turned around to listen to the red-haired prisoner's stories. I knew most of them already and I didn't care for our glances to meet. Since that Saturday night he had repeatedly made insinuating comments about Irmgard and me, suggesting that Vienna was just the right place for girls like us. And the older prisoner had kept silent; he had neither joined in, nor stopped, nor reprimanded his younger comrade and fellow-sufferer.

In the afternoon, the day after the window cleaning, two young Romanian soldiers came to the stable. Standing in the open doorway, they knocked on the doorframe and, lifting their caps, greeted us in German. On asking if they might step in, the one introduced himself by name as the garrison commandant's orderly and the other as his friend. They had come to see how we were. After a few exchanges with Gerhard, the orderly asked if they might come again. With a glance at Irmgard and me, they bowed and took leave.

Following this initial introduction, one or the other would come by every afternoon. Already the second time, one brought a woolen military blanket and special treats with him: chocolate, biscuits, dates. Sitting on the edge of the cot that I was lying on in my winter coat, the soldier would offer me these treats, urging me to try them. Quietly he'd tell me about his parents, he being their younger son, and his weekly visits to them here in Arad. He'd talk about his friend from his boyhood and school years, who, like himself, was doing military service at this garrison. Gently, he'd ask me about my family and past circumstances. As the friend of the garrison commandant's orderly, he seemed to know about our flight and objective. My answers were brief and unembellished. Speaking felt like an enormously effortful act, as did drawing my gaze lost in space to his narrow face and dark eyes. Yet, this face was soothing, almost as if the world were whole for that short duration.

One afternoon the orderly extended his parents' invitation to us five siblings to a dinner at their home, followed by a dance concert at a theatre in Arad. He quickly quieted our concern regarding permission from authorities. He had already obtained the commandant's consent. Noticing our disconcerted glance over our attire, he dismissed it with a smile.

Walking in the wintry dusk through the stately streets of Arad felt strange and as if we had suddenly been transported before a stage. The imposing houses and apartment buildings appeared unexpectedly solid and monumental, their volume pulling in on the senses like stupendous weights. The bustling city life, carefree talking, shouting and laughter, the movement and noise of traffic and pedestrians revealed us to ourselves as outsiders to normal life, and busy, everyday life seemed remote and strangely theatrical and carousel-like.

Would there be a bridge to that life again? If given it, could we, now so removed, cross the bridge and feel at home again?

I dimly remember feeling surprised by the gestures of respect, the cordiality and warmth with which the orderly's parents received us. I see us passing through an anteroom and through a room with furnishings that bespoke Eastern influence. Seated around a dinner table with linens and good china, I recall sitting across from the orderly's mother. Irmgard records that when we tried to eat the delectable food the hostess had prepared and served us, we sisters were startled to discover that we were able to eat only a small part of what had been served us; Gerhard and Puka doing a little better than we. Our stomachs had shrunk and become sensitive from our prolonged starvation, preceded by a lengthy subsistence diet. Disappointed and dismayed, we apologized to our gracious hosts, who looked concerned.

To this day I still squirm when I imagine us in our flight-worn camp attire walking into the theatre, sparkling aglow with crystal chandeliers. Following this handsome, smart-looking orderly, we, a motley lot, brought in our trail a well-entrenched stable smell. However, our young, gallant host didn't seem fazed by all this. Nor were the seats he had led us to off to the sides somewhere, but rather, in the middle of the center section of the theater. Self-conscious and apologetic, we, in turn, didn't glance around to register the other theatergoers' response. In any event, there appeared to be no audible protest. Given their Romanian temperament, their focus was perhaps fully on the anticipated, exciting dance event, or, perhaps, they had become accustomed to similar encounters in the course of the upheavals of the war and its aftermath.

As appreciative as I tried to be, I quickly wearied of the Cossack dancing. Given our emotional place and frame of mind, all the skillful leaps, foot and legwork, executed elegantly in high, shining, black boots, struck me as enormously exhausting acrobatics and incomprehensible exuberance. Nevertheless, the following day, something like smiles could be seen rising in our faces, light flickering in our eyes. This brush with life, the experience of kindness, the fresh images were reverberating. We held out hope.

Several days after this outing, the commandant stood one morning on the threshold of the open stable door, an elegant, medium figure in a splendid uniform. On his head was the officer's hat with golden braid; in his left hand, soft, black leather gloves matched his impeccably-polished officer's boots. Bowing slightly and tilting his hat, he greeted us courteously with a small, formal smile. Addressing Irmgard and Gerhard, who stood at some distance facing him, he informed them in precise, broken German that unfortunately, he had found that he had no jurisdiction to authorize, as he had hoped, our passage to Hungary. Instead, he would send us to a camp in Oradea Mare, from which German refugees were regularly transported to Austria.

Standing just a step inside the doorway, handsome and erect, he exuded gentlemanly correctness and self-respect. His ingratiating, perfect social grace suggested certain sensitivity and a refined upbringing. He wished us good luck and hoped that we would soon reach Vienna, our goal. As he glanced at Irmgard while drawing his soft, black leather gloves through his cupped left hand, a smile that seemed crisp at the corners hovered over his lips, narrowing his dark eyes slightly. Bowing, he left. I stole a glance at Irmgard. Like Gerhard, she was still standing and looking through the stable door after the commandant. The look on both their faces seemed to express uncertainty.

"*Oh, ihr habt Glück, ihr kommt nach Österreich,*"—*Oh, you're lucky, you get to go to Austria,* the younger, red-haired prisoner chanted with a grudging voice. Puka smiled. Irmgard and Gerhard looked at each other, he with his left eyebrow raised high. Then they too began to smile.

"*Na, was sagt ihr?*"—*Well, what do you say about that?* Gerhard asked, looking from one to the other.

"Wir haben Glück, wir kommen nach Österreich,"—*We're lucky, we get to go to Austria* chirped Puka, evoking a short burst of laughter from us.

"Was sagst?"—*What do you say?* Hedy wondered, turning to Irmgard, alluding obviously to the commandant as Irmgard sat down on the cot next to us.

"It was decent of him to convey the information to us directly," Irmgard responded.

After the prisoner whined, "You're lucky, you get to go to Austria" a few more times, I heard Hedy mutter under her breath:

"Wir sind noch nicht dort."—*We're not there yet.* I, on the other hand, began to feel sorry for the two, perched on the hay rack like two pathetic birds, for not being as lucky as we.

It wasn't until decades later that, touching upon the kindness and courtesy of the two young Romanian soldiers with Irmgard, I learned of the following: a few days after our outing with the orderly, he had approached Irmgard with a proposal. He proposed that he would marry her and his friend would marry me. We obviously came from a good family, and despite our prolonged misfortunes, had kept our integrity. They had wanted such girls as wives. Marrying us would ensure not only our release from prison but also that of our siblings. Dumbfounded, I asked:

"And what did you say to this suggestion?"

"I thanked him, but told him 'no,' we wanted to go to Vienna," Irmgard answered, adding after a minute: "All we could think of was our freedom. Our goal was to get to Vienna to be free. I didn't think I needed to ask you, I just said 'no.' I didn't think that you'd have chosen otherwise."

"No, of course not, but I do feel moved by their good heartedness. You know, for them to have thought well of us, despite our being just some of those thousands of refugees, our run-down appearance, and that stable smell; to respect us and want to help us. . . "

"Well," Irmgard interjected, "he thought you quite nice and pretty with your soft, brown eyes and long braids, and they obviously didn't think us to be just gypsies."

"Did he seem hurt?" I asked.

"I guess he was, a little."

I fell silent. I now remembered that he and his friend had not come to the stable toward the end of our stay there.

6

THE BLACK, BLACK WITCH

Irmgard records that it was on the night of November 19, 1946 when we boarded the train to Oradea Mare. Under the surveillance of a single sergeant, we entered the compartment to which he directed us. Though repelled by its condition of disrepair and filth, we settled on two of the better benches. Wasn't it better to be taken to Oradea Mare in this dilapidated train than to walk the long distance by foot in rain and ice? Hope kept our hearts and spirits up. As the train picked up speed and the night became even colder, a freezing draft tore through the broken windows. Big pieces of windowpane were missing. We were shaking with cold, our teeth chattering uncontrollably. All the effort at huddling together in order to ward off the frost was to no avail. There seemed no place to go; the cold penetrated and shook us like skeletons in the wind. I was gasping for breath as if my heart and lungs were choked by an icy clasp. Mercifully, we eventually found deliverance in the oblivion of sleep. Irmgard refers to this night as the cruelest of our sufferings.

The morning came, and with it, light. Soon we'd be there; the worst was behind us. The train pulled into the station. As we got off and prepared for our walk, one or the other even managed a little smile—after all, we had arrived.

Irmgard speaks of riding on a streetcar into the center of town, of our walking along beautiful tree-lined boulevards and along streets with imposing residential apartment structures. Eventually, the streets narrowed, the houses became smaller, and the pavement uneven and broken. My memory begins with the last part of that long walk through Oradea Mare, at the point when we had come to what looked like the outskirts of town: more and more isolated, low-roofed, poor and neglected looking houses; unpaved and uneven dirt-sidewalks and roads.

Something put us on the alert. No one was speaking. The air seemed charged. The sergeant was silent. He either didn't understand us, or wasn't set on answering us. Where was the camp? Where were we going? Then we turned a corner and walked up a road along a few houses. Ahead of us loomed a colossal, dark structure. As we got closer we saw its walls. Made of rough, gray-black stones, they looked massive and impenetrable. Now we made out a wall encircling the structure and, when close enough, we could see a moat surrounding the gigantic stone wall. And there was a bridge, and beyond it a dark opening: the arched entrance with its forbidding, deep stone walls that looked like a passage into darkness.

"*Eine Festung!*"— *A fortress!* I heard Gerhard say slowly, in a thunderstruck voice. Then our eyes saw the large black letters above the entrance:

ZENTRALES INTERNIERUNGSLAGER
Central Internment Camp

Aghast, we looked at each other. The sergeant standing behind us did not return our glances. Puka was the first to find words.

"*Wir haben Glück, wir kommen nach Österreich.*"— *We're lucky, we're going to Austria*, he quoted with a neutral voice the red-haired prisoner's envious chant, his eyes going from one of us to the other, lips puckered to a mocking, disillusioned smile. And the impossible happened. We all broke into a laugh. It was to be our last laugh for a long time to come.

The guard pointed with his raised arm toward the entrance gate.

"*Kommt!*"—*Come!* Gerhard said, his face ashen. We crossed the bridge, feeling like oxen being led to the slaughterhouse—passed through the shadows of the arched gate and entered the vast, enclosed inner courtyard. Again, we were in a central internment camp!

Less than a year later, Irmgard put our experience in these words:

"We came through many streets and farmers' markets. In time, we came to accept the crumbling of our illusions. But what was to follow destroyed them completely; indeed, demonstrated to us the absurdity of our childish hope, thrusting us again into wretchedness and misery..." On seeing the sign *"Zentrales Internierungslager"* above the "large gate that looked like a cold, dark cave," she writes: "Horrified and struck to the core, we looked at each other. Inside us there was the cry "I can no more, I can't go in there!... Weary, we also entered here, aware that much more difficult things awaited us. So far, we had had a glimmer of hope. It was shattered now, for who would lead us out of these walls that predicted nothing but annihilation?"

Following a brief exchange between the sergeant and the guard in the gate booth, the latter summoned a man whom he directed to take us to our room. This man, who by all appearances was a camp inmate, nodded and with barely a glance at us, led us wordlessly, with shuffling steps, across the large, cobblestone-paved courtyard. In crossing it we saw two little boys and a little girl. They had been standing in the shallow sunlight, not playing but just standing with hanging arms, looking out. As they lifted their faces and gazed up at us, I shuddered: They were vacant—large, pale and vacant. Sparse, colorless hair fell in straight, thin strands to the sides of their pallid temples.

We were approaching a tall, wooden staircase leading to a veranda on the second level, when a teenaged woman stepped out of a door and into the courtyard. Her eyes fell on Gerhard. Flashing a smile at him, she continued to smile provocatively even as she looked over her shoulder back at him while closing a door behind her. Reappearing within seconds in the company of a second woman who, like the first, targeted her brazen gaze at Gerhard, smiling as if she had already witnessed his fall. Gerhard turned his eyes away.

'Where are we?' I wondered, shaken, sensing the extent of hollowness surrounding them and staring out of their faces. Suddenly an old children's rhyme, chanted at playground games, went through my mind: *"Dreh dich nicht um! Dreh dich nicht um! Die schwarze, schwarze Hex geht 'rum."*—*Do not turn around. Do not turn around. The black, black witch is making her rounds.*

On the veranda an infirm man, looking many years older, although he probably was no older than sixty-five, pushed himself along in a narrow strip of sunshine. As one can read a once-imposing statue from its fragments, or glean the image of a once-lofty house from its crumbling structure, so one could still see in the deeply furrowed, gray face with mournful eyes and drawn-down lips the traces of the former man of stature. Struggling forward in slacks and coat nearly twice the size of his shrunken body, one felt his effort to be the exercise of a moral will pitted, even if vainly, against the hollowing power of this place that held out nothing. Was the *"Ach,"*—*Oh,* I heard coming from his lips as he lifted his gaze in passing us, a lament directed at us, the newly arrived, or was it over the misery of his own condemned existence?

Further down the veranda a young woman, perhaps in her early thirties, with a pallid face, dark brown hair pinned back behind her ears, and a long, worn cardigan over her much-too-loose dress, came out of a room. Leaning over the wall of the veranda, she called down into the courtyard:

"Karli. . . you're a good, little boy. . . aren't you? You're playing nicely with Rudi. . . aren't you?" There was no echo coming up from below. As she turned, she saw us. Something flickered up in her care-worn face. Our guide had stopped three doors down from the woman.

Turning toward us, the woman said, "My name is Tilda. If you need information or something. . . you know. . . I live here." She quickly pointed to her door. We thanked her.

The guide pushed open the door further down.

"There, that's your room; you can go in here," the man said in a monotone voice, barely looking at us. Turning, he shuffled toward the stairs leading down into the courtyard.

Frozen, overwhelmed by the realization of where we were and what we had seen, we stood behind the closed door. After all the hardships and misery, and our ever-new hope and endurance, we ended up where we had begun. Betrayed!

What met our eyes was so repelling that we didn't want to take one step beyond the threshold; grimy walls with large cracks and holes, and bands of bedbugs plastered along the cracks. The floor was filthy and littered; dust and old straw scattered all around. Broken windowpanes, crusted with years of dirt. A huge heating oven, its masonry walls streaked with soot, from which cold air was blowing into the room. In the absence of wood, lighting, and fire, the oven's function was seemingly serving its purpose in the reverse. A broom stood in one corner, worn to a stump. Along the wall to the left of the door stood a narrow table and a bench. Without saying a word, we finally took a few steps into the room and, feeling infinitely weary and overwhelmed by the situation, sat down.

Hours passed in total silence. It was there and then,

I believe, that for some, if not all of us, the solitary plunge into the well of darkness had begun. In time we would come out of this darkness with a new faith and trust, on the strength of which we would walk out of this mighty fortress and invincible bulwark. Following his visible devastation in those first hours inside the fortress, Gerhard re-emerged as our leader. Different. He seemed older, calmer, and surer; as if with a new center of gravity. He was the first one to get up and set to cleaning the room, as well as to orient himself to the camp. When he returned with a pile of newspapers, a broom, and bucket, the four of us were still sitting motionless and silent. He proceeded to sweep the floor, throwing the old, smelly straw and debris into the bucket, which he emptied several times somewhere outside. Then he crunched up the paper, stuffed some into the holes of the broken windows, and the rest into the heating oven.

"Perhaps we'll find some twigs and branches somewhere and make a bonfire to warm up the room. In the meantime, it should be a bit less drafty in here," he said looking over to us with a little smile that was meant to encourage and give us hope. He then washed the floor with cold water that he retrieved a number of times from the pump in the courtyard, using a rag that he had borrowed from Frau Tilda. At least two of us would have to sleep on the floor.

Gerhard had learned from Frau Tilda that beyond one meager bowl of thin soup a day and an occasional piece of bread or dry polenta, there were no other food provisions for the camp inmates. Nor was there wood or coal with which to warm up rooms or cook. However, there was straw in some stable lofts with which one could start a fire in the oven and heat up the room. Of course, one could also use the straw to sleep on.

So how did people survive with this starvation diet, and how did they get through the icy winter days and nights? Those, he learned, who still had some money or objects of value, such as a wedding ring, family jewelry, or a fur coat could exchange these for money to buy food, while inmates with contacts—such as relatives or friends on the outside—could receive food and some money.

And who were these prisoners in this fortress? Many were ethnic German Romanians, who, like those in Yugoslavia, had been disowned and imprisoned. Others were ethnic German refugees who, like us, had been caught and placed here. No one knew of any transports that had been taken from here to Austria, and the majority had been held here for more than two years.

It was freezing cold inside our room, and it did get colder as the winter progressed. Yet, we heated up the room only once, at the tail end of our time at this fortress. The decision not to make a fire in the heating oven was reached within a few hours of our arrival, for it had occurred to Irmgard and Hedy that the warmth would bring to life all the bands of bed bugs plastering the walls. That the place abounded with fleas and lice, which would spring to life with a little heat, we didn't doubt. This disgusting image mobilized us. At our sisters' mention of this, we quickly rose and moved the table and bench further from the wall.

Gerhard and Irmgard were wondering whether they should try to exchange one of the two silver coin ducats, hidden under the inner soles of Hedy and Irmgard's shoes ever since leaving the first shelter we'd found with the farmer couple in the Romanian village. There was a knock on the door. Frau Tilda was bringing us some warm food—hot polenta porridge with a sauce.

"Just a little something for your hunger. You didn't even get today's soup," she said shyly and apologetically in her German dialect. Infinitely grateful and shy in turn, we thanked her. It was the first food we had eaten in more than thirty-six hours. The small tin bowls and spoons she had brought with the food we returned that evening, rinsed clean. Gerhard and Puka had groped their way down into the large courtyard, barely lit up with a couple of low-voltage bulbs, and rinsed them clean under the running water of the pump.

The first night as in the nights that followed, we

sisters took turns lying on the table and sitting on the bench. The one sitting up would lay her head on the table, cushioned on her forearm. Gerhard and Puka slept on the floor. Hoping to find and preserve body heat, we lay and sat close to each other, limbs tightly pressed against the body. But sleep often proved elusive and fitful: Icy shivers, hunger, and nightmarish visions of what awaited us in this fortress held us in their grip.

Within a few days, Puka and I were chosen by the camp authorities to clean offices several times a week at the Oradea Mare gendarmerie. Going down the veranda and crossing the courtyard always made me feel apprehensive, as I never knew what faces and images of misery and hopelessness I might encounter. The children's rhyme, "Do not turn around! Do not turn around. . ." would on these occasions come to me, as if to warn me of danger.

Our walk to the gendarmerie in town took us past the daily farmers' market. The mounds of bread, baskets full of crisp rolls, of green- and red-cheeked apples, garlands of smoked sausages draped over rods and hooks, never failed to stop and engage us—even though, or precisely because they were not in our reach, and we were so hungry. Hunger made us fantasize, imagine, and circle around food as the lover's thoughts might circle around the image of the beloved from whom she was separated. There were vivid memories of food and piercing regrets over past food left uneaten or passed up. Once or twice it happened that a clerk at the gendarmerie coming back from his lunch brought Puka and me a small bar of chocolate or a fresh roll from the bakery. Shyly, gratefully, we would put them in our coat pockets, to immediately pull them out once on the street to consume a portion, and then joyfully treasuring the rest to share with our sisters and brother.

One day Gerhard asked if we had seen any maps in the offices. Yes, there were two large maps on the wall in one office. One was definitely of Romania. During the time the clerks were out for lunch, Puka and I now began to take turns studying the maps and keeping watch, both feeling equally anxious and nervous. It had been made clear to us that anything beyond sweeping of floors, emptying of wastebaskets and dusting of desks and chairs was forbidden territory. We never got beyond the large colored map on which we had indeed, after much searching, located Oradea Mare as well as the Hungarian border running close by. Regarding the second map, we could only report that it bore the city's name in big letters. At this news, Gerhard's face lit up with a sly, expectant smile.

Under one or another pretext, Irmgard and Gerhard managed to temporarily fill in at the gendarmerie for Puka and me. Within a few days, they had gathered from both maps the information they had hoped to find: the location and approximate distance from Oradea Mare to the Hungarian border west of it; the western-most sector of the city and the streets leading from the fortress through that sector; names of Hungarian villages and towns closest to the border. Beyond the happy confirmation that we were only some twenty-five kilometers east of Hungary, Irmgard and Gerhard also discovered that the river, Crisul Repede, running through Oradea Mare, was flowing in a more or less direct line westward through Hungary, where it eventually flowed into another river. It promised to be our surest signpost guiding our steps to freedom.

Not that I took particular notice at the time, of all the information my sister and brother had gathered. Irmgard's later reference to Puka and me sitting for hours in the same place and position, often not even lifting our heads or eyes to their departure or return, refers to this period of our captivity in the fortress. We resided for long stretches of time in a solitary place of darkness and silence. From here we'd emerge briefly, as it were, to go to our work, fetch and eat our meager daily bowl of soup, partake in the devotional Gerhard might call us to, or when someone addressed us directly. Most of the time we did not exchange words.

The Winds of Fortress Kula

The decision to escape and flee to Hungary became more urgent with every day. Gerhard and Irmgard had broached the subject and we all understood the compelling reasons for it. Each of us knew that it meant taking enormous risks. The possibility of failing filled us with terror, causing us to shrink back. And yet, the prospect of staying held equal terrors, as it held out nothing but living death; hopeless degradation. We knew that if we wanted to preserve our selfhood and willpower, we had to act before physical decline and demoralization had fully set in, disabling and paralyzing us. And yet, the dread of all that awaited us out there loomed large: rain, frost, homeless days and nights, trekking through unknown lands, never-ending roads, feeling lost, hungry and exhausted; the ever-present danger of renewed imprisonment and being turned over to Yugoslavia.

In the coming days, fear lifted its warning scepter inside me. I would see black masks and puppet heads on bronze billets hobbling slowly across a stage, bobbing, turning, and nodding. Flashing up with glistening glow, they'd bow while looking back at me from beneath their lowered brow mockingly, revealing for seconds their features to me. Gasping, I'd recognized in them the faces of the ghost-like existence at this fortress, one with neither hope nor future.

7

"OUT OF THE DEPTHS DO I CRY"

We would not attempt to flee until we had gained confidence, Gerhard assured us. Confidence? Confidence that God would lead us out of this fortress and guide us to our goal.

And how were we to come by this confidence?

In the early afternoons or before dark Gerhard might read aloud passages from the pocketbook Bible, a Lutheran translation; with the soft black leather cover—the one he had pulled out of Father's large, triptych-like bookcase the last time he had broken into the family home. He'd read from Paul's letters to the Romans and Corinthians, as well as from the Psalms by King David. He was bound to have read also from the Gospels; such as Matthew, chapter 6—inviting the reader to trust in God's provision and care, giving the birds and lilies as examples. One of these times he read the words of the Psalmist:

"Aus der Tiefe rufe ich, Herr, zu dir. Herr, höre meine Stimme. . . "—*Out of the depths I cry unto thee, O Lord. Lord, hear my voice; let thine ears be attentive to the voice of my supplications. I wait for the Lord, my soul doth wait, and in His word do I hope."* (Psalm 130:1, 2, 5.) Long familiar to me, these words now struck. As if dropping into a shaft inside me, hitting the walls with sparks of light, they reverberated as chimes of bells reverberate within the space they break into.

In the ensuing days they silently echoed inside me, gathered dispersed and unconscious energies until the psalmist's cry became my cry, my prayer, my waiting. In those hours and days of waiting with my eyes, like doors closed to the world, my father's image and parting words would come to me. Tall, in his black winter coat and hat, he stood near the corner of the internment camp where a group of selected women and girls had gathered to be taken to an unknown labor camp. Hedy, Irmgard and I would be among them. The carts that would transport us were already waiting. Father had taken leave from Hedy and was taking leave from Irmgard. Before stepping in front of him for my leave-taking, I glanced back at Mother standing across from us, holding Claudi and Waldemar close to her. Claudi, not yet twelve, willowy and tall, was taking in everything. Waldemar, a little over four, in his light blue winter coat and matching wool cap, was holding onto

Mother's coat while watching the scene and looking up at her with an uncertain and worried look. For she was gazing at us; pale, and quietly crying. Taking both my hands and pressing them against his chest, Father looked at me lovingly and sorrowfully, uttering these parting words:

"Dora, mein Kind, denk daran, dass Gott unser höchstes Lebensgut ist. . . "—*Dora, my child, remember that knowing God is life's highest good. He may call and encounter us on many different paths and in many different ways. Perhaps the path you're now entering will be the one he'll meet you on. May God bless you and keep you safe, my child, and may he sustain you."* Bending over me, he kissed my cheeks and forehead.

One day, while standing in line with my bowl for my serving of soup, there arose within me the words: "You're being guided." Surprised, I listened. "There's been guidance," the inner voice continued in an infinitely light way.

"This? Guidance?. . . All this?"

"Listen; take notice. . . " the inner voice said gently. I noted the lightness with which these words had risen into my consciousness, and how they seemed to be written in light. "Take them in the way a child would hold the tender feather that has floated into her path in her cupped hands."

I now gently coaxed myself, only to return skeptically:

"O, yes, unless ye be like children. . . " But catching myself I turned and said, "I will take them as a gift and hold them close in my spirit. I will try to trust them and remember them." And as I moved and stood there in the courtyard, I was aware of feeling light and as if something in me had shifted.

Increasingly, and for longer periods of time we would feel calm and peaceful following Gerhard's devotionals. A new trust was growing inside us. And one day we were ready: We reached the decision to flee.

It was a Friday afternoon and the time was set for Monday, December 2nd. Saturday afternoon, we lit the bonfire in the heating oven. While a large pot of water was getting warm, the worst of the chill in the room was also taken off. One after the other took turns having a sponge bath behind a borrowed sheet, which served as a curtain. It and a tin washbasin were borrowed from Frau Tilda. A small piece of soap and two clean strips of sheet completed the toiletry. Refreshed by this luxury, we felt gently buoyed and energized. Irmgard suddenly suggested that Puka tell us the story of Franja's abduction of him from his prison camp. Puka's eyes lit up with interest. He was looking at the rest of us, who nodded in agreement, saying:

"Ja, ja, Puka erzähl mal."—*Yes, yes, Puka, come, tell us.* Encouraged thus, he showed himself quite eager. Smiling expectantly, we got up and moved the bench

and table closer to the oven to catch the last rays of warmth from its walls. As he sat on the table, we, on the bench before him, listened spellbound to the amazing story that Franja had told him and Gerhard as they hurried through the dark streets to the house of the two women guides.

To orient Puka and set the stage for his narrative, Irmgard now briefly recalled: "The women pressed for setting out, but you hadn't come yet. And, of course, we couldn't leave without you. And we worried, not knowing if you were lost or something had happened to you; or if you were unable to get out of your camp. So Franja offered to go to your camp and try to abduct you. We were skeptical and had misgivings about his safety. After assuring us that God can work wonders, he did a little performance impersonating a person of authority; like a secret agent or a military or police officer, which had all of us chuckling—even the two women".

"That's him, that's how he was," Puka grinned, eager to recount Franja's story of his abduction.

Arriving at the entrance of the wing of the town's garrison that was now prison to some fifty local German men and boys appointed to do forced labor as a city painting crew, Franja identified himself to the camp guard as being commissioned to fetch prisoner Eduard Drumm. The reason he gave was an interrogation at the local headquarters of OZNA, the Secret Police. Meeting with reluctance on the part of the guard to hand over one of his charges without the authorization from his own superior, Franja next told him that he was a secret agent charged with the responsibility of procuring said prisoner for interrogation regarding two other prisoners, and regarding his own possible implication in this matter under investigation. As the guard was still balking and skeptical, Franja assumed an impatient and authoritative pose and tone, observing that he didn't have time to stand around waiting, and that comrade so-and-so should please oblige him by heeding orders from superiors.

This tone and reference to superiors appeared to have the desired effect, for the guard was now eager to reassure Franja that he, of course, wished to comply with orders from superiors—but that in light of no orders from his immediate command or any document to that effect, the sir comrade would surely understand. Encouraged, Franja took another stab at cooperation by asking with a still higher pitch of impatience and authority, whether the comrade really meant to imply that he should identify himself? Reaching with his hand inside his coat, as if intending to get out a summons from his inner coat pocket, he casually, and with a conspicuously irritated, nasal voice inquired about the guard's name. At this, the guard protested with:

"*Nje, nje, gospodin komerad. . .*"—*No, no, sir comrade, it's just that my duty requires* . . . He saluted and turned to fetch Eduard. When the guard, who in the meantime had called on a second fellow militiaman as a witness, brought him out, Puka was going "Fra...!" with surprise and recognition in both his face and voice.

"What happened then?" we asked with apprehension and as with one voice.

Puka continued, "I guess his eyes and voice stopped me in time from going on, as did his voice and command, when he declared that prisoner Eduard Drumm must at once follow him to the headquarters where the authorities were delayed in conducting their interrogation. This cut short all further protest on the guard's part." Puka's exclamation had set off renewed suspicion in the guard, moving Franja to shout his resolute command and quickly retreat with his charge.

When Puka came to the end of the story of Franja's incredibly ingenious and courageous rescue mission, we looked at each other, nodding and smiling. Some may even have laughed for joy. For the story served to buttress both our resolve and newly-found trust. Astonished, we realized that although that night felt already so remote, separated by so many experiences, it had actually taken place a little over two weeks ago.

8

A RIVER AND A STAR

Monday, December 2nd had arrived. Irmgard, Puka and I stayed in, while Gerhard and Hedy went to work at the gendarmerie. We were to meet them sometime after noon in a side street that Gerhard had designated to Irmgard. In the days we had spent in our room at the fortress, we had learned to tell time by the progression of sunlight both indoors and out. When we gauged the time to be noon, Irmgard looked at Puka and me.

"Ich glaub es ist so weit,"—*I think its time to leave*, she said. The two of us nodded in agreement. Visibly paler, we got up, and holding each other's icy, trembling hands, we stood for a moment in silence. Collected, we opened the door and walked onto the veranda. We exchanged greetings with a few women and girls standing in the sunshine. I felt them looking curiously, if not suspiciously, at the three of us dressed in our coats and head covers. Calmly, we went down the stairs,

purposely talking to each other. We needed to look and act natural, in order to not arouse suspicion.

There were a few people in the courtyard. We were walking toward the gate. Glancing back, I saw that the eyes of the women on the veranda were following us. Two girls were leaning over the wall, as if to see us better. Were they suspicious? Would they shout, striking alarm or would they remain silent and not draw the gate guard's attention to us? We were near the gate. To its left was the guard's hut. It was empty. The guard wasn't standing on duty, neither by the gate nor in the hut. My heart—though racing—leapt for joy. I could have laughed. Calmly, holding my breath, while something inside me was dancing, I passed with my siblings through the cold, vaulted dark gate; crossed the bridge spanning the moat, and took the road that would lead us to the streets toward the open. It was a bright, crisp afternoon out there.

A little past the farmer's market, we turned into a side street. Gerhard and Hedy were not there. First the three of us stood waiting, but as time wore on, we decided it safer to walk several blocks up and down the street, with Irmgard and me on one side, and Puka on the other side. Time wore on and our anxiety grew. Irmgard began to wonder if we shouldn't return to the fortress. At least all of us would meet there and attempt to leave again another time. In that case, we should take no chance and return before our absence had raised suspicion.

As we were considering this course of action, Gerhard and Hedy turned the corner. Cautiously, Irmgard and Gerhard exchanged signals, whereupon he and Hedy turned again and we followed them from a distance. While near the center of town, our path took us along streets bustling with people talking, and activities that struck us as ever-so-remote and surprising, showing us—even more than that time in Arad—how removed we were from ordinary life. Coming through quieter streets, we picked up our walking pace; eager to get into the open and gain a good head start toward the Hungarian border before dark. The threat of gendarmes looking for us lurked in our minds as a constant danger.

Before long, we were to have a near-encounter which could easily have been our undoing. In walking across one of the city's several bridges spanning the river Crisul Repede, we espied our fortress gate guard coming toward us leading a cow by a rope. In his free hand he was holding a newspaper that he was reading. Praying that he might not recognize us amongst the other pedestrians, we continued to walk. And indeed, he did not look up but passed us by, his attention totally engrossed in what he was reading. How immeasurably relieved and thankful we were.

We were on a road beyond the outskirts of the city.

Through an underpass we could see a long stretch of fields. With a surge of energy we hastened inside the underpass. As we stepped out we froze. Running parallel with our underpass was a second underpass some twenty yards to the right, with two guards standing watch. They were checking people on their way to the city for identifications or permits. Gasping, we quickly retreated back. Frightened, we wondered what we should do. Gerhard even considered a quick, cautious retreat with the intention of trying to leave the city from another, less precarious exit point. After a pause of weighing our options, Irmgard turned, and, pointing with her head toward the fields ahead of us, proclaimed:

"Wir sind unter Gottes Schutz!"—*We are under God's protection*! And with this, she walked resolutely out from the underpass with the rest of us following her lead. We could see the guards looking over at us, but they neither stopped nor called out to us. Were they only watching for persons entering Oradea Mare and not for those leaving it? Or did they actually not see us, even though they appeared to be looking at us? We didn't know. To us it was like a miracle. I counted it as the third one that day.

Once we were out of their sight, we eagerly sped up our walking pace. Gerhard was looking for the road leading to the river. We had been walking for a long time and we were getting tired. At last, out of the vast silence, we thought we could distinguish sounds of water. We stopped and listened. Yes, all five confirmed that, intermittently, we could hear flowing water. Seeing in our mind's eye already the river and its bank, we excitedly turned leftward toward the source of the sound, with renewed hope. But before we had reached the riverbank, we found ourselves walking on soft ground, which soon became wet and slippery. We were beginning to wade through mud. Here and there we caught glimpses of glistening black waves. Our longed-for guidepost turned out to be inhospitable. The alarmed screeches and whirring flutter of the startled wild fowl rising from their nests confirmed what we had begun to fear: We had landed in a marsh.

Indeed, Irmgard and Hedy were already surrounded by reeds reaching over their heads. Hedy was calling for help. Ankle-deep in water, she was unable to pull up her feet without leaving her shoes behind. Gerhard had to come to her rescue. Cautiously, we made our way back onto solid ground. Here we continued in what we hoped was a forward push. Weariness, cold, and hunger began to weaken us and weigh on our spirits. But carrying the vision of our faith before us like a sacred banner, we tried not to become despondent. Thus, we advanced slowly. Gerhard, who vigilantly looked for a road leading to the river as well as for signs indicating the Hungarian border, kept up a steady pace. The four of us followed him at a slower pace, with Puka and me trailing behind the others.

Coming down the gentle slope of a meadow, we beheld a herd of sheep huddled together under the cold night sky. Two tall figures looking like lone statues against the darkening, wide horizon, stood motionless in long, stiff sheepskin coats that reached to their feet. A cylindrical hat of the same stuff as their coats crowned their heads like a bishop's miter; low over their brows. These two shepherds with tall staffs planted on the ground, stood watch over their herd of sheep in the freezing winter night. As we got closer we greeted them, hesitantly waving our hands as one does when meeting a hiker on a mountain trail, or when greeting a neighbor across the street. They returned our greeting. Their eyes followed us as we passed them. Yet, we felt no fear. Instead, I felt as if I had passed by a still-point, a benign, timeless presence, or one of those luminous saints in old icons that flicker up on their dark, cracked canvas amidst the candle light and clouds of incense and the incantations of supplication: *"Bože ... dragi Bože ... saslušaj nas ... usliši naše molitve!"*—God ... dear God ... hear us ... hear our prayers!

To my sisters I said, "They didn't seem at all hostile."

Irmgard agreed, adding, "And I'm sure we're not the first wanderers who have passed them looking for the Hungarian border."

"They have it good; they're nice and warm in there between the fur and leather. No wind penetrating those. And their feet... up to the knees in fur," observed Hedy in a plaintive voice.

"And they're familiar with the surroundings and find their way in the fields, while for us, it all looks the same," Gerhard threw out over his shoulder, sounding a bit discouraged. Agreeing with him, we now drew in our necks and shoulders even more; as if our worn coats suddenly provided even less cover against the cold and wind.

I vaguely remember that when passing the shepherds, Hedy—who still knew Hungarian from the days we had lived in a Hungarian community—called out to them:

"Hol van a Magyar?"—*Where is Hungary?*

They responded by pointing with their arms somewhat diagonally in the direction ahead and slightly to the left.

"Köszönöm!"—*Thank you*! Hedy and Gerhard had called back, joy and gratitude filling their voices.

We felt as if we had been walking endlessly in the direction indicated to us, without having seemingly come any closer to our goal. There was no sign anywhere of a road, river or road sign—nothing to point the way.

"We must have inadvertently been walking toward the right," concluded Gerhard. "We have to try to get back on course." But how were we to determine that course? Scanning the land and sky, he and Irmgard consulted with one another. In the end, they decided to choose a large star that shone brightly ahead and to the left of us as our compass. We all had noticed it when looking in the direction in which the shepherd's arms had pointed. I remember us walking toward the star, lifting our eyes again and again to see this point of light in the late evening sky.

We had been trekking along steadily, if also slowly, when we were overcome by such fatigue and sleepiness that we felt we could not continue without some rest. Although Gerhard must have craved it as much as the four of us, he worried about the prudence and safety of such a rest stop. We'd be putting ourselves too much at risk, he argued; both because we might be very close to the border and thus border guards, and because of the wet, icy ground. Hearing his reasoning, Irmgard at once joined ranks with him. Together we formed a close circle and, falling on our knees, we fervently prayed for strength and help, aware, as Irmgard was to formulate it, ". . . that only our faith could help us." Rising, we continued through the night; our eyes set on the star in the sky, our hearts harkening back to the trust with which we had begun this journey.

Thinking that we had been walking forever and must, therefore, be near the border, we felt on the alert and began to anxiously hold our breath. Suddenly we saw a house lit up in the near distance. Ducking, and with hurried steps we made a large detour around it. Coming across a patch of tall grasses, we hid in it, mainly to allow Hedy and Irmgard to put their dislodged attire and shoes in place. No sooner did we lower ourselves to the ground, than Puka and I promptly fell asleep. I remember Gerhard shaking us by our shoulders, whispering urgently to wake up, for we had to go on; there was no tarrying. It was too dangerous. Able to only halfway tear ourselves from the delirious clasp of sleep, we begged with tears for understanding and compassion; and when he refused, we began to accuse our persistent older brother of heartlessness and inconsiderateness. The indescribable craving for sleep—to which Irmgard admits as well—became the seductive lure of a Lorelei, promising the sweetest satisfaction in the surrender to the yearning. It was Gerhard's wakeful persistence that saved us from succumbing. With her moral strength now boosted by Gerhard's willpower and reasoning, Irmgard became his ally in overcoming our resistance. Between conjuring up terrifying images of the consequences for remaining on such uncertain, danger-filled territory, and sweet words of encouragement, she got Puka and me to rise and start out anew.

The lit-up house was no longer in view when we suddenly heard the rabid barking of dogs. Then we saw a wavering, flashing light as from a swaying lantern. Suspecting that we were near a farmhouse, we quickly hid in a nearby ditch. With heads ducked and hearts pounding we listened. The ferocious barking was coming closer. The dogs were headed in our direction. We feared the worst: that these savage sounding dogs were tracking us down and would pounce upon us, attacking us viciously. But a sharp whistle suddenly sliced through the air, causing them to reverse their direction. The barking soon ceased, and neither light nor steps were approaching. Relieved, but with limbs feeling drained of all blood, we lingered in silence.

"Well-trained dogs. . . thank God!" whispered Irmgard after a while.

"Yes. . . luckily!" responded Gerhard, adding after a bit, "We were really lucky. . . not bitten and not discovered."

"*Eine Landstrasse,*"—*A country highway,* I heard Irmgard whispering excitedly.

"*Wo?*"—*Where?* We whispered back as we lifted our heads to peek. We saw a paved road lined with trees that beckoned us to the possibility of a village nearby. Energized by this prospect, we climbed up the bank, wondering which way to turn. Which direction would lead us to a Hungarian village rather than a Romanian one? We decided to turn right, fervently hoping that it was the direction that we hoped for. But Irmgard and Hedy found themselves unable to walk. Their legs were seized with painful cramps. First Gerhard, then all three of us set to rubbing their legs. Leaning on us and supported by our arms slung around their backs, they eventually fell into a pace again, their sobs slowly giving way to smiles.

Before long, we were certain we were approaching a village. Through the silence we could hear the distant but clear sound of barking dogs and church bells ringing.

Entering the village, feeling both excited and apprehensive—not knowing where we were—we saw two men coming out of a house. We greeted them in Hungarian with a "Good morning." They responded in like speech, but with "Good evening." As agreed in advance, Hedy asked which country we were in. "In Hungary," they answered. At this good news we became jubilant. For the moment, all fatigue and the dispiritedness was gone.

We further learned that it was nine o'clock in the evening; that we had, in fact, already crossed over the border into Hungary (that we were actually three kilmoeters in); that the road we were on led directly to Budapest; and that Budapest was 248 kilometers to the west. As with our experience at our first border crossing, we were again incredulous to learn the actual time of day. To us, the past eight to nine hours seemed to have spanned a lifetime. On the other hand, in our elated state, the 248 kilometers to Budapest appeared to us to be but a matter of a few hours away; an easy feat in light of the arduous and dangerous challenge we had just put behind us.

What childlike optimism we felt! It buoyed our resilient hearts and spirits, enticing us to enter upon uncertain paths with naive confidence. There, by the entrance to the village, our hope was effervescent. We were exhilarated—we were in Hungary!

We knocked on many doors seeking shelter, but none was opened to us with hospitality. We continued marching along the road we had so happily come upon, reminding ourselves that this village was probably still too dangerously close to the border, anyway. Our joy and gratitude being great, we were at first able to keep our disappointment and weariness at bay by marking the kilometers we were putting behind us; by reiterating to ourselves the proof from both past and recent days of what good hikers we were, and by reminding ourselves of the odds we had overcome through our determination and faith. We recalled how we had feared that at Christmas we'd still be in the dreadful fortress in

Oradea Mare, imprisoned and without hope. Now, we pictured ourselves in Vienna by Christmas, celebrating in freedom.

By and by we fell silent. Fatigue, cold and hunger began to gnaw, threatening to overwhelm us. We had walked forty kilometers, and our bodies sent signals that we were reaching the end of our reserves. We came to another village. Knocking on windows, Hedy and Irmgard begged for modest shelter—a stable, a barn, or just a haystack. But in vain. In one instance, Irmgard and I had gotten as far as a farmhouse kitchen outside of a village. While putting forth her plea, following it with explanations of our plight, bringing into play our mother's Hungarian origin, the birth and youth of both of our parents under the Austro-Hungarian aegis in the province of Batschka; yes, their schooling and fluency in the Hungarian language, the farmer continued sinking his teeth into the meat from a roasted chicken thigh and chewed noisily. With greasy, smacking lips, he then proceeded to suck out the marrow from the bones he was breaking with his teeth. In the end he threatened with a gesture to set his large, shaggy sheep dog against us, causing us to hastily depart. I remember Irmgard's voice trembling with outrage. "So heartless, so merciless, eating like that in front of us, our begging—but scaring us away..." We retreated to the road. It was in reference to that night that Irmgard noted in her journal that the road seemed to have become our home.

Icy winds swept unchecked over the vast, flat fields. The fabled Hungarian steppe we had encountered in songs and literature met us in its bleak and deadly cold stare. Thirst had joined our hunger. Wells with buckets hanging from tall poles, so characteristic of the Hungarian countryside landscape, stood against the dark horizon like lone hospitable emblems of life. Yet we couldn't get near them to quench our thirst; for large, ferocious dogs guarded these wells, keeping wanderers from trespassing. Slowly, we pulled ourselves along. With interlocked arms, Gerhard and Irmgard on either end, we braced ourselves with bodies bent forward against sweeping, freezing winds. Inevitably, we would catch ourselves nodding off, our heads drooping to our chests, then starting up.

Again, some of us, including Irmgard, were begging for sleep. Gerhard warned against it. "Not with the frost on the ground and nothing to shield us." We went on, with me crying quietly and Puka and Irmgard whimpering from time to time. We came to a white road post: "Budapest 200 km." We stopped.

"So, Dori, you sit here," Gerhard said pointing to the post. At once Puka and Irmgard dropped themselves to the ground next to the post, leaning against each other, succumbing, like I did, instantly to sleep. In the meantime, Gerhard stood in front, shielding us like a shepherd from the icy wind and harm. The craving for sleep had become our most dangerous adversary. Hedy, who knew that she couldn't afford to sit or stand still, was pacing back and forth crying softly to herself.

Within five minutes, Gerhard aroused us. Unrelentingly, he ignored our pleas for a few more minutes of sleep. Didn't we know that we would freeze to death? "Yes," Irmgard admitted, attempting resolutely to get up from the ground. But her legs had become so stiff and numb that Gerhard and Hedy had to help lift her up and support her as she took some steps, crying after each one.

Again we closed ranks and slowly pressed on, fervently praying that we might come upon a shack or hut. From my half-awake state I recall Puka suddenly calling out:

"Eine Hütte!"—*A hut,* and seeing in the field a short ways to the right of the highway, a white hut gleaming in the dark. Our eagle-eyed little brother was once again the first to have spotted one. Running down and then up the shallow ditch on the roadside, he raced across the field toward it. Looking through the open doorway inside it, he waved to us:

"Kommt, kommt!"—*Come, come,* he called out, cupping his hands around his mouth. As we got nearer he shouted joyfully:

"Come, come, we can sleep in this one."

The Winds of Fortress Kula

"Are you sure?" Gerhard called back, remembering, as we all did, the broken, muddy shack of our first night. It was a small hut with no door, filled with dry grape wines. We dropped down. Turning on one side, there was room for four. Puka lay at our feet. There was no grumbling about the hard bedding or sticks poking us. And despite our chattering teeth and trembling bodies, we quickly fell asleep.

Puka's voice awoke us. It was daylight. Lifting my head, I saw him standing outside the door, holding in his raised hand a single long winter root vegetable as a hunter might hold a hare. Small clumps of dirt still clung to the sides of the long tail-like root. Steam rose from his nostrils and open lips as he looked at us excitedly with a grin that betrayed a face stiff with cold.

"Where did you get that, or should I say, where did you steal that from?" Gerhard asked with half a laugh while the rest of us tried to sit up. We were moaning, for our limbs were stiff and every movement hurt. The vines we had lain on now poked us sharply. Always an early riser, wakening with dawn and the crow of roosters, Puka had slipped out of the hut while the rest of us were still wrapped in sleep. Scouting about the immediate surroundings, he had come upon a little garden patch with winter root vegetables, not far from the hut.

"There are more, but I only took this one," he said. We understood and nodded. Our hearts were filled with gratitude toward the owner. We felt that we had somehow transgressed already, by sleeping in his hut. But our hunger was so great, we decided to take this one. Passing it around, each took a bite until the root was gone. As Irmgard noted, this was the only meal we would have that day. The ten little apples Gerhard had brought for our flight had to be saved for still greater hunger.

When the four of us tried to stand up and walk, we found our joints to be stiff and every uncertain step so painful that we felt as if we had to learn how to walk again. This was not too surprising, as the fields were white with hoar frost, and we had slept in the open hut with no covers other than the clothes we wore. Nevertheless, we returned to the road with renewed courage and energy. And before too long, we were able to walk at a moderately reasonable pace again.

Gerhard proposed a new plan that made Budapest our immediate intermediary goal. We'd try to get to Budapest as quickly as possible. By putting sixty kilometers a day behind us, we'd be there in three to four days. An uncle of our mother, great-uncle to us, lived in Budapest. The pastor as well as director of a Methodist hospital, he would take us in, provide us with rest and food and if need be, with medicine, having in his earlier days also been an apothecary with his own store. Finally, once rested and restored, he'd arrange for our transportation to Vienna. Even given the hard post-war times, this great-uncle Jani Tessenyi, Jani Batschi (Uncle Jani), as we called him as children, was bound to have resources and connections to assist us in these ways. Thus went our brother Gerhard's reasoning.

It didn't take much persuading on Gerhard's part to have the rest of us agree to his plan. The sooner we could get into a home, get warm, rest, sleep and food, the better. That Budapest didn't lie in a straight line to Vienna but indicated a certain detour didn't concern us. It was better in any case to be on a road that led you in the right direction, than to wander around muddy and frozen fields not knowing your way.

The preceding night's experience had demonstrated the daily threat that the severe winter cold posed to our health and lives. Obviously, we could not count on being given shelter and food, nor could we continue going without rest or sleep. And it was obvious that our physical strength and endurance were rapidly diminishing. As it was, Hedy and I were skeptical about being able to do the projected daily sprint.

After a few hours, the optimistic back and forth exchanges with which we had started out on the road in the morning were beginning to wane. At the same time, our walking pace was slackening. Then it began to drizzle.

It took longer and longer to come to another milepost indicating the remaining kilometers to Budapest. Our spirits threatened to sink, but were quickly boosted again by a kind Hungarian farmer who, driving in the direction we were heading, offered us a ride. Delegated by Gerhard as the liaison person—a choice the rest of us unequivocally supported—Irmgard sat on the front seat with the farmer while I, being the smallest, was chosen to sit in the middle. The other three were sitting inside the open cart. Guessing our situation, the farmer asked about our destination, with questions Irmgard tried to understand and answer the best she could with the little she and Hedy remembered of Hungarian, and with help from the farmer's minimal knowledge of German.

In the meantime, the drizzle had turned into rain. Whether prompted by the rain and his own kind heart or by the little he had been able to glean of our dire situation, the farmer went out of his way and drove us to the next village. Here, we climbed off the cart with smiles and many *"Köszönöm!"*—*Thanks!*—while he, wishing us good luck, turned around and went his way.

It was pouring now. Rain was running down our drenched head covers, hair and faces. We could feel the wet chill penetrating our coats. Irmgard and Gerhard knocked on many steamed-up windows, asking for shelter. But the housewives, busy and flushed from standing over their stoves cooking the family luncheons, shook their heads with one or two *"Nem, nem,"*—*No, no,* quickly drawing their slightly opened windows shut again. One woman told us to go to the Red Cross located in the next village.

We gave up knocking on more windows pleading for shelter. It was hard to have to beg and be constantly rejected. At the same time, we could hardly fault the people. There were not just two or three of us, but five, and our current down-at-the-heels appearance doubtlessly didn't inspire particular trust. Irmgard and Gerhard unequivocally decided against seeking help from the Red Cross, fearing that word about us would get to the police. They decided that instead, we would go to the train station close by. Despite her broken Hungarian, Irmgard had managed to find out from the friendly farmer who had given us the lift that the closest railroad station was located in the next village. Had she already concluded that a train ride was our only recourse to make it to Budapest? In any case, while walking in the downpour the twenty kilometers to the next village, feeling cold, wet, tired and weak from hunger, we made the train station our goal; a hoped-for refuge. We'd be out of the rain and cold, and sooner or later would board a train that would take us—if luck was with us—to Budapest in a mere few hours.

Of course, we had no money. Did we have moral qualms about our plans to ride the train without tickets?

I do not remember. I do, however, recall fearing being caught, taken to task, and turned over to the police. Our situation was desperate. Only determination and endurance, coupled with resourcefulness and helping hands on the way, could promise us survival. Gerhard, in any case, raised no questions and showed no signs of conflict of conscience. His decisions were, of course, influenced by his sense of responsibility for all of us.

It was late afternoon when we reached the train station. Irmgard and Gerhard quickly figured out from the posted schedule that the next train to Budapest was leaving this station at 2:30 in the morning. Fearing possible inspection and that our appearance would attract attention, we chose to sit outside the entrance rather than in the waiting room. Soon, however, a railway guard stopped and questioned us. Though Gerhard and Irmgard withheld what would incriminate us, he seemed to guess our situation; and moved by kindness rather than the letter of the law, he led us to two empty benches inside the waiting room, urging us to sit down on them. We didn't know yet that huddled groups of refugees outside of train stations was a common sight in many post-war central and southeast European countries, and thus a sure giveaway. The waiting room was heated. Sitting on wooden benches rather than on cold, wet ground was so blissfully comforting that we leaned against each other and fell asleep.

The Winds of Fortress Kula

As discussed beforehand, we boarded the same compartment but in separate groups. Hedy and Puka, as Irmgard and I, squeezed onto two different benches. The compartment was crowded and not all passengers found a seat. Gerhard ended up standing in the aisle, in order to avoid being addressed by others. The four of us who were seated either pretended to be dozing or lost in our own thoughts by staring fixedly out the window into the dark. Irmgard was clasping my hand, squeezing it reassuringly from time to time. The train was speeding through the night, while our hearts beat fast with both joy and fear.

In time, the conductor came and asked the newly-boarded travelers for their tickets. His voice sounded gruff. It was, after all, 2:30 a.m. He appeared to take his task seriously, carefully checking and punching the tickets before returning them. Irmgard was holding my hand tightly. We tried our best to look assured, as if we had passed the ticket inspection at an earlier time. The four of us on the benches were lucky. Gerhard was less fortunate; a good head taller than the men around him, he stood out. Too conspicuous to be overlooked, the conductor had good reason to assume that all those standing in the aisle were newly-boarded passengers. The conductor made a commotion, demanding that Gerhard, along with any other ticketless defrauders, disembark at the next train stop. When the train rolled into that station, the four of us followed Gerhard and stepped off the train. Standing again in the cold and dark, we wistfully looked after the train that was rolling out with whistles, picking up velocity as it sped into the night to its scheduled destination.

"We are, at any rate, two villages ahead," Puka said with a faint grin on his pale, thin face. Shivering, our shoulders drawn up to our ears, we nodded at Gerhard who looked at us with eyebrows raised questioningly and lips puckered, as if to say: "Here we are again, now what?" For lack of a better solution, we decided to stay till daylight in the station waiting room, where we'd escape the cold and would hopefully catch more sleep till dawn. Little did we know how fateful every turn and our timing would prove to be.

The morning came and we returned to the highway. Tormented by raging hunger, we each ate the last small apple, slowly and reverently as if taking a sacrament. The fields were white with frost and the road with a treacherously slick layer of ice.

"Be careful, be careful not to slip and fall," Irmgard warned as we gingerly watched the ground and our steps, arms slightly raised as if to better balance ourselves and ward off skidding. Trying to boost our spirits, we remembered the kind railway guard and recounted the previous night's train adventure, highlighted the twenty-some kilometers head start we had, and chuckled about our nerve and the conductor's heated outrage at Gerhard trying to get a free ride, unaware that there were in fact five of us. Soon, however, walking became so difficult, and our progress so slow, that we began to have serious doubts about our ability to make the 170 kilometers to Budapest.

We now came to put all our hope on some kind of transportation, be it farm cart, car or truck; observing that it was this targeted hope that helped us to keep on going. I can see us moving along the highway that morning as if on a leisurely stroll, each walking at a different pace; the pace each could muster. Gerhard, then Irmgard, would call out encouraging words aimed at our striking a faster pace, while we others would mutter, "I'm already walking as fast as I can."

I felt lightheaded. Irmgard would from time to time put her arm under mine and with *"Komm, Dorchen!"* draw me gently along. In turn, Gerhard would assist Hedy. Most of us had swollen feet. I had large painful blisters; some had been rubbed open from the holes in my stockings. Thus we were trailing along like a "beaten army," to quote Irmgard. Yes, that's how we looked and that's how I remember the retreating German army trekking through our town in the summer of 1944, weary and beaten on their way from the Russian front. Their wounded and weak lying in slow drawn carts crawling along the bumpy cobblestone-paved streets. No guns displayed, no smart goosesteps in shiny boots, no songs as in 1941: *"Führer befiehl, wir folgen dir"*—*Führer command and we shall follow.* Only here and there, wane smiles on weary faces with sunken eyes, a feeble wave of the hand at the wide-eyed children standing on sidewalks taking this in, waving back shyly, and remembering.

9

THE RUSSIAN TRUCK

It had begun to drizzle when we heard the oncoming sound of a heavy motor behind us. Turning, we saw a Russian military truck. All five of us waved for it to stop, but it drove past us. We kept waving. Not long after we had dropped our arms, feeling sad and disappointed, the truck suddenly came to a halt. Not on account of us, but on account of a car that lay in the ditch along the highway. We were less than one kilometer away. The two Russian soldiers got out of the truck and inspected the site. As with a bolt of lightning, new hope and energy went through us: "This is our godsend opportunity; we must run and get to them before they take off," we said. Eagerly and desperately, we all tried to run, but not everyone could match her intention. I, for instance, got no velocity into my run, no matter how hard I tried, and Hedy lagged behind me.

"*Geht! geht!*"—*Go!, go!* Gerhard waved and called to Irmgard and Puka, who were in the front ranks. Taking Hedy's and my arms, he pulled us along with him. Oh, that they would not leave before we made it to their truck, each fervently hoped and prayed. And behold, putting every effort into the last sprint, we reached them as they got into their truck and before they had shut their doors. At the steering wheel sat a Russian soldier; in the passenger seat an officer. We stood looking up at the officer, pleading. Pleading for a lift. We were on our way to Budapest, would they please give us a lift, even if it were only to the next town, even one or two villages down the road, or just a few kilometers. We were cold and tired, the way was long, and we couldn't walk any longer. We all knew some Russian from the occupation days and so each one would raise his hands and plead. The driver looked straight ahead, expressionless, with his eyes fixed on the road ahead of him. The officer looked at us and at the driver. Then the driver started up the motor. All our hope resting on a ride, the five of us instinctively ran and lined up in front of the truck and with raised hands pleading, *"Pozhaluysta! pozhaluysta!"*—*Please! please!"* The motor was running at an accelerated speed and we didn't move out of the truck's way. They won't run over us, a voice said inside us.

Finally, the officer turned to the driver. He must have told him to let us get up on the truck, for the driver got out and motioned to us. With smiles and repeated *"Horošova"*—*Thank you,* we climbed into the back of the truck. We happily counted the road posts and kilometers flitting past us.

"Hey, look!" Puka suddenly called out excitedly. With one hand he was holding up the lid of a bare wooden barrel, while his other hand held a handful of pickled green tomatoes. A few bites and he had them down. Though chiding him, the rest of us nonetheless followed suit, blind with hunger. After two or three helpings we suddenly broke into an embarrassed laugh, let down the lid and sat back on the truck floor. No one wished to repay the officer's help in this way. I remember seeing the officer looking back at us digging into the barrel and eating. Yet, he didn't rebuke us or put us back on the road. Perhaps he understood that ravished hunger can be more powerful than good upbringing, social etiquette and a well-entrenched conscience.

At one of the towns, the truck exited the highway and stopped in front of a small restaurant. "It must be noon and they are stopping for a warm meal", we thought, "or maybe they're going to drop us off here and drive on." How incredulous we were when the officer invited us to join him and the driver for a hot lunch.

Shyly, we entered the restaurant and sat down at the table with them. He ordered seven servings of hot soup and a very substantial entrée with meat, bread dumplings, gravy, and cooked cabbage. If by chance, he hadn't surmised the extent of our ravishing hunger from how we had fallen over the barrel of pickled green tomatoes, he certainly would have guessed it from the eager concentration with which we devoured the soup, then turned to the servings on the plates. When we'd look up and express our appreciation with a little smile, he might meet our eyes, nod and express his satisfaction. He seemed to be studying us or to be weighing some thoughts.

I have difficulty now, recalling the officer's face. Dimly, I see a well-cut, firm face. Tall, strongly built, and no older than twenty-eight or thirty, he wore his rank and authority in an easy manner, with no swagger.

The driver remained detached. His head and broad shoulders bent over his food, leaning on his forearms resting on either side of his plate, he occasionally glanced at us, betraying no involvement, no empathy, no hostility. What was expected of him by training and custom was following orders and carrying out missions; not taking sides or making decisions.

When we had emptied our plates, the officer started to ask questions. Where were we headed? To Budapest on foot? Since when had we been on the road? Where had we been spending the nights, and where would we be doing so?

With an almost exasperated voice, he asked, "Do you realize that in this freezing winter temperatures you'll freeze to death? On foot, in your condition, you won't make it to Budapest. You'll die on the roadside, freezing to death," he prophesied unsentimentally.

Almost apologetically, Irmgard and Gerhard explained that we realized the gravity of our situation, but having no other recourse, we were trying to make it to Budapest where we had an uncle on whose help we could rely. After a short silence, the officer turned to the driver and said, *"Etat djeti"*—*They're children*. The driver nodded in agreement. Looking at us across the table, the officer told us that they would be passing by Budapest on their way to their destination. They could take us along and drop us off at Budapest. We'd be there well before dark.

At first we were dumfounded and speechless at such unexpected and unimagined good fortune, as well as at the generosity and kindness that it bespoke. But after a bit, our faces beamed and our spirits were soaring. All our worries appeared to be gone in the face of such a turn in fortune and goodness.

The officer suggested that Irmgard sit in front with him and the driver in order to discuss matters further. On Gerhard's and my not unselfish urgings, she reluctantly followed the officer's invitation, though not without resentment.

"It's always me who has to do the talking and negotiating," she complained.

"It's just that you're so good at it," Gerhard responded appealingly, with a brotherly teasing voice and smile.

Inquiring about our uncle's address, the astonished officer learned from Irmgard that we didn't have it.

"You don't? It's a big city, you know," he observed.

"I know that," our sister, always an all "A" student and well-versed in geography, threw back. "I know that it is a cosmopolitan city with some two million inhabitants. It won't be difficult to get the address of the Methodist Hospital in Budapest and once we get there we can easily contact our uncle," she explained.

"I see. So, he is associated with the hospital. Is he a doctor?"

"No, he is not a doctor, he is the director of the hospital."

Before long, the officer had also learned that our initial and ultimate goal had been Vienna. That we were now trying to get to Budapest was only because of our desperate situation. Perhaps a bit amazed himself at this coincidence of converging goals and circumstances, the officer now admitted that actually they themselves were on their way to Vienna. Thus it happened that he declared himself willing to take us across the Austrian border and on to Vienna.

"Getting you all across the border will be a little difficult; we'll have to hide you," he pondered more than once.

Oh, how unspeakably happy we were at this news which Irmgard, opening the front window, called to us four sitting in the back. We hugged each other, laughed, felt astonished at this stroke of luck—no, at such amazing providence. How we flew past road posts, trees, and houses, waving at Budapest; like a bride bejeweled in her white winter dress beneath the blue sky and pale golden sunlight, sparkling between her shimmering streams. High-spirited, we waved goodbye to her as we hastened past, rapidly pushing forward, conquering kilometer after kilometer.

His voice resonant with joy and wonderment, Gerhard pondered: "As the saying goes, when the need is greatest, God's help is nearest."

Nodding, Hedy added in her unsentimental way: "Yes, and He needs many good people." Gerhard didn't disagree with Hedy's addition, but nodded thoughtfully. Our glances shifted to the front compartment of the truck.

Shortly before dark it began to rain. With no roof or cover over our heads, the four of us couldn't help but get wet in the back. Though uncomfortable, we kept our cheer, imagining where and how it would be if we had to walk through the night in the rain, hundreds of kilometers behind. Huddling together, we put our heads between our drawn-up knees, stood up our coat collars, and were silent or dozing, letting out startled shrieks when we'd suddenly feel rain trickle down our necks.

The driver knocked on doors and windows in the villages we drove through, asking for shelter for the night—but in vain. Who wanted or had room to put up seven people, and strangers at that? At last we stopped by a small, forlorn-looking house that stood by itself on the roadside. Light was coming through the simple curtains. A couple opened the front door. They immediately said "Yes," and warmly welcomed in all seven of us.

An old woman appeared, taking at once our wet coats and head covers to dry by the stove, while the wife beckoned us to come closer to the stove to get warm from the rain and chill. After a while, the officer invited everyone to sit down and help themselves to the food he had unpacked and laid out: an astonishing spread of rare cheeses, pâtés, and other such delicacies that made the five of us gasp, and must have seemed quite fabulous to our hosts as well. It was evident from their one-room dwelling that they were quite poor. The husband worked as a road sweeper. They were Russians. The couple's two children sat down with us on the straw that the husband had brought in and spread on the floor for his seven guests to sleep on. Five ethnic Russian Hungarians, two red Russian military, and five ethnic German refugee youths sat and ate together.

In the morning, the officer was more reserved. He told Gerhard and Irmgard that, regretfully, he could not take us with them directly to Vienna, after all. The border inspection, he explained, made it too difficult in daytime. He could take us only to the last village this side of the border. We should go there for shelter and rest awaiting the dark for the final stretch to the border. "The villagers will take you," he assured our siblings. As a last piece of advice, he warned against walking on the highways or roads from here on, as we would be too visible. From now on, we were on dangerous terrain. Border guards on both sides were on the lookout for refugees and others wanting to get across without passports or authorization. We should walk where we wouldn't be conspicuous and, if possible, stay camouflaged. Somewhat embarrassed, Gerhard and Irmgard thanked him repeatedly for all he had done for us.

In due time, the truck pulled to the side of the highway to let us off. Nodding his head, topped with a fur-lined cap, the officer indicated a country road leading directly to the main street of the village, while wishing us good luck and nodding to our words of thanks. The Russian soldier quickly smiled at us as he opened the door to get back in the truck. Was he trying to convey that he felt a connection? The truck sped off toward the Austrian border, leaving a trail of steam behind in the cold morning air. We hastened down the bank onto narrow field paths bordering the country road; along ditches, past shrubs and trees, which despite their bareness might screen us from direct view.

To find ourselves on the road again after Vienna (and with it, safety and freedom) had seemed in such imminent reach, was, of course, sobering and disappointing. Not that we didn't know and appreciate all we had gained and been given through this remarkable, caring young Russian officer. We were now hundreds of kilometers ahead on our journey; our ravished hunger was, for the moment, sated; we had been given warm shelter, rest and sleep, we had been treated as human beings by our "enemy." We were back on the road that morning feeling restored enough to feel that we could make it to our next goal.

We didn't talk much as we wound our way along the shrub-lined paths through the fields. No one touched on the officer's altered plan and reserve. We felt that we understood his reasons, and we felt sad.

When on the previous evening the seven of us were ready to settle down for our night's rest, the officer wanted Irmgard to lie next to him in order to discuss with her, as he explained, the next day's plan and strategies. Passing quietly over the officer's wish, Gerhard lay down next to the officer instead. Directed by his eyes and almost imperceptible pointing of head, Puka took the place next to him, I next to Puka, Irmgard lying down between Hedy and me. After all had fallen quiet in the room, the officer voiced his wish again, addressing Irmgard directly over all our heads. Again, his words were met with silence. She, as the rest of us, appeared to be wrapped in deep sleep.

"They're asleep already from all the exhaustion and loss of sleep. Better tomorrow morning, officer," Gerhard had whispered with an appeasing, conciliatory, and pleading voice.

A sunny, blue sky stretched over familiar-looking white stucco houses. Silvery smoke rose from chimneys on rooftops into the crisp, midday sky, conjuring up images of farm wives by large wood stoves cooking dinners for their husbands, children and live-in elderly parents. Like the houses with the deep-set windows, neatly trimmed, the sidewalks and streets were clean and intact. Walking a little distance ahead of the others, Irmgard and I expressed our astonishment at this picture of undisturbed community life. Was it possible that war and strife had passed it by?

Knocking on the door of one of the larger houses, a pale yellow corner house on the sunny side of the street, we at once were warmly and hospitably taken in by the farmer couple whom we had asked for shelter until dark. At the onset of dusk the farmer, who appeared to be in his early forties, accompanied us through the village to the open fields. Though he didn't know the way to the border, he knew, he said, that we needed to keep steering leftward. As he turned back and we moved forward, I couldn't help but wonder about the risks to him and his family in helping us.

Near the outskirts of the village we had come across a man. The two men had greeted each other with *"Guten Abend,"*—*Good evening.* Glancing at the farmer's face from the side, I noticed no fear or unease. Could it be, I wondered, that these villagers had the assurance of having no informants amongst them; that they lived within a community of trust, free of fear? I hoped that it was so.

10

ARE WE IN AUSTRIA?

Referring to our setting out on this, our last crossing, from Hungary to Austria, Irmgard notes that "... this time we were calm and peaceful, for we had prayed... and our souls were weary." I do remember feeling calm and being aware of the calmness in the others. And while we were all affected by a profound and pervasive weariness, the miraculous turns in the last two days uplifted our spirits, hope, and trust. We were nearing the end of the long road. We expected that once on Austrian soil, our fears and hardships would be over. The bond of German ethnicity, certainly in light of the persecution we had suffered on account of it, assured us refuge and safety.

And so we went into the night with collected spirits. Not long after we set out, it began to rain. The night was dark and walking was difficult. We were walking through freshly-tilled fields. With each step, we were sinking into rain-drenched soil. Irmgard and Hedy were constantly losing their shoes, which, tattered and worn, would get stuck in the mud and slip off their feet. Slowly, we were moving closer to the border.

Streaming rain obliterated the surroundings. Remembering the farmer's advice, we kept to the left, which, under the given conditions, was difficult to gauge. Glimpsing suddenly a light in the dark, we took a sharper leftward course, figuring that it might come from a border guard or surveillance lighthouse and that once we passed it we'd be on Austrian soil. After a long span of arduous and numbing trekking through clinging wet soil and meadows ankle-deep in water, we stumbled onto a country road. At once our senses were awake again, as if we had emerged from oblivion.

I see us standing on the road, looking around; Gerhard and Irmgard wondering which way to go and how we might determine on which side of the border we were. Although it seemed impossible, it now rained even harder. I still can see the rain coming down, as if in white sheets. It was as if the skies had opened their floodgates, dropping oceans of water onto the earth. Gerhard decided that he and Puka would follow the road to one side, in the hope that it might lead to a highway and thus to some clues as to where we were. As they took off, we sisters drew closer. With our heads lowered, shoulders drawn in, our lower arms raised and pressed against the body, we stood as if to ward off the onslaught. But there was no warding it off. The rain was coming through; we could feel the cold wet on our skin, the water in our shoes.

Standing there like this, lifting my eyes to this bottomless downpour and impenetrable darkness, the image of cattle came to me, standing in the night in rain and cold—defenseless, enduring.

Our brothers returned. They had come on neither a highway nor any other clue. We decided to follow the road in the opposite direction, when after a few steps a male voice shouted:

"*Halt!*"—*Stop!*

A bright, blinding beam of light shone at us through the rain and dark. We stood still. We could hear the sound of heavy boot steps coming toward us. And now, we saw a tall figure in militia uniform; one hand holding the flashlight, the other the leather strap of a gun hanging from his shoulder.

"*Sind wir in Österreich?*"—*Are we in Austria*? Irmgard called out, barely able to contain her triumphant joy.

"*Ja,*"—*Yes,* the young border guard called back.

"*Gott sei Dank!*"— *God be thanked!* The five of us exclaimed as if with one voice, with boundless joy and relief that came from the bottom of our being. We were laughing and might have fallen on our knees with thanksgiving, but for the torrential rain and presence of the guard. All was forgotten: the wet, the cold, the weariness. We felt happy as if we were facing a friend, not an enemy. But the guard had his duty. His job was to intercept illegal border entry. Hence he had to come to business: What country did we come from, what was our citizenship?

"You will be sent back to your country," came the verdict.

"Wir sind Volksdeutsche."—*We are ethnic Germans.* "They put us all into concentration camps, we escaped, have been on the road—" Irmgard tried to explain.

"I am sorry, but that's the law. Whoever enters the country illegally, will be sent back to their country."

"Then shoot us right now. Better to die now than to be sent back. After all we've gone through, in winter, on the road in rain and ice, day and night, through two countries. . . to get here, where we thought we would be free—!" she exclaimed, her voice resonant with bitter dismay.

"Yes, better to die now, they will kill us anyway; they torture the ones who are caught," Gerhard echoed our sister.

The guard had listened. Was he moved, or did his duty leave no room for human consideration? We should follow him, he told us. He had to take us to the station for protocol. On arriving at the headquarters, he led us into a room with a huge, white masonry stove flanked by two benches at either side. We should sit down and warm ourselves; they would call us in a little while, he told us before leaving the room.

How we hugged the thick, warm walls of that stove! What comfort its slow, even warmth gave us. Like a mother, it let us lean against her sides, embracing her temperate body heat.

Shortly, two other young military guards came in. *"Guten Abend,"* they greeted us. they then asked a few questions, which reflected their curiosity. Seeing us shiver and chatter with cold, they suggested we remove our drenched coats and hang them near the stove for drying. Of course our clothes were wet too, but at least this way they had a better chance of becoming less so.

It was perhaps nine-thirty in the evening. With the great fuel shortage in the post-war years, the fire in the stove had been allowed to die down for the night. As the walls spent their stored heat and the room became cooler, we clung to the cooling white walls to soak up their last remnants of warmth. One of the young militiamen returned carrying apples and slices of bread in his hands; one for each of us. We must be hungry, they thought. Regrettably, there was no warm food around, he apologized.

For the protocol we had to walk through a cold and brightly-lit hallway to one of the offices. I remember windows on the left side of this hallway, and how I shuddered seeing rain slashing against the windowpanes, turning into foamy, white little streams against the black impenetrable night. Oh, that we might not be thrust into that night again! How good it was not to be out there!

The guard who had apprehended us took down the information. We could see the sense of outrage rise in the faces of the young border guards as they heard about the demise of the ethnic German Yugoslav population at the hands of the Yugoslav communist government. The news of its first programmatic persecution and genocide of one of its ethnic minorities had obviously not yet penetrated to the outside world.

Back in the room, the oven walls were now cold. The guards came in with two or three blankets; horse blankets as they were called, coarse and scratchy but thick and warm. Folding them around us, we could feel our shivering slowly give way to drowsiness. Given our childish hearts that clasped onto every promising sign, we were overcome by tiredness and sleep with a glimmer of hope. Our young Austrian captors had been empathetic and kind to us. We had gotten this far; would we be forsaken now?

Irmgard writes that we slept fitfully that night, starting up from frightful dreams and extreme cold. As the night's temperature dropped below zero, the single woolen blankets provided an inadequate shield for our weary bodies swathed in wet shoes and clothes.

I see us walking out on the highway leading to Vienna. We're feeling hopeful and cheerful. For the present, we're not thinking of the long distance to our goal; nor the winter, the rain and cold, snow and frost; nor of our weariness and chill—our clothes and shoes are still damp, and it is raining—or how we will sustain our strength; where food and shelter will come from. We are joyful, for we are free and walking on Austrian soil. We can speak openly and no one will be suspicious of us on account of our speech. For the time being, we are filled with gratitude and confidence.

When the morning had come, the guard who had apprehended us at the border informed us that in light of what they had learned, they reached the decision not to return us to Yugoslavia but to let us continue our journey to Vienna. For seconds we stood there speechless, looking at the three young guards with wildly joyous faces, while they, looking pleased, smiled back at us. Alternately, Irmgard and Gerhard expressed our profound gratitude to them, while they in turn wished us good luck. Anxious that we should have a safe and good start, one of them led us past the nearby village and onto the highway whose northeastern route led to Vienna. A milepost read: "Vienna 63 km."

For the protection of our three kindhearted young Austrian border guards, Irmgard did not record the incident of that morning. It was clear to her, as to the rest of us, that the route taken past the village rather than through it was as much for their protection as for ours.

Irmgard also did not mention the shelter we were given the following night in a village by an ethnic German refugee woman on whose window she happened to have knocked. This woman opened her door welcomingly to us though we were five strangers, dripping wet and with muddy, torn shoes. In coming years Irmgard would remember this woman, preserving her story for me, who had no such recollection—her sons' beds in which she let us sleep, the linens on them as impeccably clean as the white curtains on the little windows of her small house; her rationed food she shared with us; her worry about our wringing wet coats, safety and wellbeing; and her own sorrow. In the eighteen months since the end of the war, she had received no word from either her husband or her two young sons, drafted into the "Wehrmacht" just months before the end; she desperately hoped that strangers in Russia or Poland might give a helping hand to her sons or husband in need. And finally, Irmgard recalled how this woman's experience of resentment from the villagers led to a feeling of isolation, because she was an outsider. Irmgard did not record these stories, because of her concern that the lives of these people might be put in jeopardy.

Taking leave the following morning from our kind hostess with much gratitude, we returned to the highway. We were of good cheer, although it was drizzling. After all, we were in Austria and had slept in comfort, eaten, and our clothes were near-dry. Soon however, it turned into pouring rain. But before long, a truck stopped and two Russian soldiers offered us a lift. Amiably, they chatted with us and inquired about our destination, telling us that but for a brief detour a few kilometers down the road, they were heading in the direction of Vienna. Our goal was Bruck an der Leitha, Gerhard and Irmgard said, and we wanted to get off the truck three to five kilometers before the town. Bruck an der Leitha was on their way, the Russian soldiers explained. They could drop us off there, they repeatedly offered. But Irmgard and Gerhard unwaveringly insisted that we wanted to get off before Bruck an der Leitha and walk ourselves to the city. At the designated point we started our march, and they turned to the right on their mission.

Advised of the border checkpoint at the gate of Bruck and der Leitha, Gerhard and Irmgard seemed to think that there was less risk of detection when on foot, mingled in a crowd mostly made up of locals routinely passing through on their way to work in the town, than in a military vehicle invariably subject to inspection. A well-reasoned plan but for one unlucky turn that would take us down a different road.

The Winds of Fortress Kula

It was raining lightly now. We were approaching the town. The three oldest were walking some eighteen meters ahead of Puka and me. They had already passed the checkpoint, with a tall Russian guard on duty. They were now waiting for us. Puka and I approached the checkpoint; our hearts were in our throats. Suddenly, we glimpsed a slighter male figure standing halfway between the guard and our siblings, gesticulating agitatedly in a back-and-forth exchange. Now fixing his eyes for the first time on us, he called out loudly,

"Aha! Come, you! I can see that you belong together, that you're of the same sort."

"Let them go, just let them go... they're young... just children..." the Russian guard tried to persuade his colleague in his broken German.

"Nein! Schau, Zigeuner."—No! Look, Gypsies. "We've got enough of them already. They came here illegally," retorted the other in fluent German. As he was gathering up all five of us into a parked police car, the Russian guard made one more effort on our behalf, but to no avail. We were about to get into the vehicle to be transported by our captor to the local border guard headquarters, when a truck stopped in the middle of the road. The two Russian soldiers from earlier shouted to us to come and get up on the truck, to continue our trip. We smiled hopefully at them, all too ready to go with them.

"*Nein, nein!*" our captor protested. We had no visa; he was taking us to the headquarters for interrogation.

"But they have been traveling with us, and we left them off a ways back while we had to carry out a task. Just let them, we'll take them with us," the two soldiers appealed. But the zealous Austrian guard wouldn't hear of it, he had to follow *"das Gesetz"*—*the law;* it was his *"Pflicht"*—*duty* to hand us over to the border headquarters. Lifting their arms helplessly and shaking their heads, the soldiers looked at us regretfully, and waving a greeting with the words: "We're sorry... good luck!" they drove off. Filing into the guard's vehicle, we wistfully looked after the truck speeding off.

The five siblings in a park in Vienna, 1947. Left to right: Irmgard, Gerhard, Hedy, Eduard, Dora.

Based on our vantage point, Puka and I had quietly concluded that our bedraggled appearance and the fear written on our faces had led to the checkpoint incident and the subsequent incarceration of all five of us. Strange to say, I learned only recently that the sequence of events had been actually somewhat different: The three older siblings had passed the checkpoint unhindered, when several yards beyond it, they were stopped by the Austrian guard with: *"Halt! Halt!"*—Stop! Stop! He had spotted them from his car. The absence of IDs or passports confirmed his suspicion that they were not legal residents. Ready to take them to the border guard headquarters, Irmgard and Gerhard informed him of their two approaching siblings. Apart from the fact that this recent revelation freed me from any residue of self-blame, it also explained what had perplexed and surprised me at the time: why the three were standing so close past the checkpoint facing us, and their faces bearing the sweet, resigned smiles rather than reproach. Once again, there had been no questioning or blaming between us. Each did his best and we stood together as one.

11

WHAT ELSE?

Following a brief protocol at the headquarters, we were taken to a local prison and led to a small room by our prison warden. The room was just large enough to hold two narrow plank beds—one being a bunk bed—and an enclosed latrine that was open at the top. A fairly large window with iron bars on the outside looked onto a small courtyard. Sizing up things with a quick glance, Puka remarked dryly with a wink at the yard and a mocking smile in his deep-set eyes:

"We'll probably be allowed to promenade daily out there a bit, so as to keep fit and to manage our cabin fever."

"How informed you are. Wherever did you get this knowledge from?" quipped Gerhard with raised eyebrows and the mere suggestion of a smile on his disappointed face.

"Oh, well, one just gets around in the world."

Although glad to be together in the same room, even if the room was very small, we were stunned and feeling humiliated. On taking one hard look at us, the suspicious prison warden pronounced us to have lice. He was sure that we had lice. Owing to this discovery or to suspicion, we were all placed in this little cell "in order not to infest other inmates."

"Was noch?"—*What else?* Irmgard said bitterly after the warden had closed the door, turned the key, and walked away. Her face and voice reflected deep repulsion. To her, it felt like the final stamp of degradation.

Following several quizzical and distrustful glances at the not-too-inviting blankets that covered the plank beds, we sat down: we sisters on the side of the bunk bed, our brothers on the opposite side. What else could we do? Before sinking into our own inner thoughts, Puka managed to come up with another little quip:

"Ihr habt Glück, ihr kommt nach Österreich."—*You're lucky, you get to go to Austria.* Instantly, the image of the two war-prison escapees perched on the hay rack rose before our eyes, causing us to burst into a laugh that quickly took on the color of comic irony. Looking at Hedy, I quipped:

"Sind halt Pechvögel."—*We're just an unlucky bunch.*

"What else?" Irmgard had uttered bitterly and with revulsion after the warden had left us locked in this small prison cell in the town of Bruck an der Leitha.

As we were soon to discover, there were indeed other experiences awaiting us here—priming us, as it were, for those still to come.

We were held in this prison for nine or ten days. With the exception of a few colorful incidents and images, the days we spent here bear in my memory the feeling of vacuous sameness. The disappointment and disillusionment that must have been there for us would have been coupled with the terrible numbing and dulling effect of our confinement and the monotony it brought. We sat for long stretches of time in silence, each captive to his or her own thoughts, dwelling in a cloudy inner landscape. I don't remember having to lie down or rise at a certain time. I'm sure we welcomed the dark, when we could creep under the blankets and give ourselves over to sleep. I do not recall scheduled mealtimes, just meager servings at dusk of either a boiled potato, a thick slice of boiled cabbage, or a bowl of soup; always hopelessly inadequate to appease our hunger. Our brother, Eduard, also recalls a daily allotment of bread that the warden would throw into our cell through the barely opened door, indifferent to whether it landed in our outstretched hands, onto the repulsive blankets, or on the floor. Hunger, the waiting for, and thinking of food, increasingly filled our days and thoughts. Our hunger was such that it drove us on a few occasions to supplement our starvation diet by "stealing" food that, we were certain, was intended for us prisoners but was withheld by the warden.

All but Gerhard had returned one afternoon from our promenade in the little courtyard, while our tall brother continued to walk in circles and diagonals, looking calmly but inquisitively about.

"Schaut was ich hab!"—Look what I've got! he said secretively and with a triumphant grin, as he came into the room and placed himself in front of us; pulling from his coat pockets several large, warm, boiled potatoes.

"Wo hast du die her?"—Where *did you get these from?* We wondered, feeling both scared and delighted, biting hungrily into them before he could give an answer.

"Aus der Wanne."—From the tub.

"Aus der Wanne?"—From the tub?

"Yes, from the tin tub next to the wall around the corner of the house, where the kitchen door is. The tub was more than half full and ready to be fed to the pigs. I'm sure that they were delivered to the warden for the prisoners. Instead, he lets us starve and fattens his pigs."

With Gerhard's discovery and plausible explanation, some of us managed once or twice to secretly sneak one or two of these steaming hot potatoes into our coat pockets, devouring them skin and all with good conscience in the secrecy of our cell.

One afternoon, Irmgard returned from her promenade in the courtyard to the cell with a new find. Her face was lit up with a happy smile. In her hand were a few pages of a magazine.

"Well, what have you got there, looking so pleased and excited? No potatoes today?" queried Gerhard teasingly.

"I saw them on a chair by the kitchen and asked the warden if I could look at them. He gave them to me because, as he said, he didn't need them anyway," Irmgard explained with a happy voice.

"So what does it say, has the Austrian government decreed to give amnesty to the ethnic German refugees whom they're keeping locked up, or has Tito perhaps—?"

"It's not about politics, it's about—they list—"

"I bet I can guess," interrupted Gerhard laughing. "It's about literature, art, and the theater."

"So? Yes, they list various cultural events in Vienna and reviews of performances and new publications."

"You and your culture, no matter what!" Gerhard laughed again.

Looking hurt, Irmgard retorted: "At least it's something that lifts one out of this endless morass. All this time, all these years... unending sameness: no news, no newspapers, nothing about the world." Our sister asserted this with indignation and dignity. She, who from age twelve on, spent all her free time at the city library; who at thirteen had Father's permission to help herself to the classics from his bookcases; and who at sixteen saved spare money to buy art books.

"I can't wait to finally—" she came back once more with an impatient look, stamping her foot defiantly. I looked at my brother:

"Gerhard, please...!"

"Igat, I was only teasing you," he appealed with a rueful smile. She was expecting good things of Vienna.

Sunday had arrived in Bruck an der Leitha. The afternoon sunshine was coming through our barred window, creating the illusion that its bright winter light was warming up the room. Gerhard had conducted a devotional, and our spirits felt lighter. Sitting as usual on the beds across from each other, we were talking. Recalling certain episodes from our journey, we naturally came to draw certain parallels and contrasts. The latter quickly led to humorous subjects, and even giggles. Gerhard, with tongue in cheek, had touched on the subject of "dutifulness" of, say, a Serbian or Romanian official vs. an Austrian or German one. This quickly got our younger brother to ask:

"Can you imagine a Serbian or Romanian border guard going out in that downpour to patrol the border in the black of the night to make sure that no little refugee was sneaking into his country?"

"A Serb? No, no, and a Romanian probably not either," we responded snickering.

"Not enough of that Kantian-Protestant sense of duty in the blood of those Slavs and Romanians," added Irmgard. Naturally, the next example to suggest itself was the Austrian checkpoint guard, whose dutifulness had landed us in the prison we were sitting in.

I now interjected: "He threw himself on us with such zeal, and how different he was from the Russian guard, who urged him, 'Just let them go, they're children.' But no, he—you'd think that being Austrian and having been defeated he'd—and here was the Russian, the enemy and victor, being more lenient, and showing more heart." I believe it was at this point that Gerhard, with a more thoughtful than impassioned expression, told us that the Austrian border militia received thirty Schilling for every intercepted head.

"We were quite a catch, then!" Hedy remarked, while Puka gave a short, loud whistle. Looking wide-eyed from Gerhard to each other, we all fell silent.

Not long after this little carefree and sobering interlude, we heard steps in the corridor, then a key being pushed into our door and turned. The door opened. In the doorway stood the warden with two disheveled looking men in dark, crumpled, baggy suits and white shirts that were buttoned to the very top but missing the customary removable, starched collars and ties. The men were olive-complexioned, had dark hair, and looked sheepish; even if not particularly sensitive or educated. The warden made it clear that they were to share the room with us. "Where? In this little room?" our eyes must have asked. Pointing to the right side with the two single plank beds in bunk-bed style, he explained in his local speech:

"You can be on this side and they on the other."

"And sleep?" several of us involuntarily wondered with startled voices. Shrugging his shoulders the warden pronounced pacifying and confidently:

" 's wird schon gahn."—*It's gonna work ok.*

To share the little room with one's brothers was different from sharing it with strange men. The arrangement with the latrine was especially disconcerting to us sisters. Why were they put with us? Were all the other rooms already overcrowded or did the warden suspect them to have lice too? Irmgard suggested that he probably wanted to put all those "Mediterraneans" together. Holding her two fingers discretely to her nose, she soon asked Gerhard with urgency in her voice to please open the window.

"It's cold. Do you want it to get still colder?"

"Don't you smell it?" Irmgard asked annoyed and repulsed.

"Yes, garlic... so?" Gerhard responded with an impish smile.

"Yes, and fish and Wurst, and beer or Schnapps. Please open it." They had whispered this exchange, figuring that whoever trafficked in Austria probably knew some German.

As we were to learn soon, the two new jailbirds—both about thirty—were quite curious and willing to talk. In broken German (our sister and brother's conjecture proved to be correct), they asked why we were here and where we had come from. As for themselves, they were Italians. "Not far from your home country; your next-door neighbors," they explained.

"From the southern or northern part of Italy?" Irmgard wanted to know, observing that we came from the northeastern part of Yugoslavia. They came from the south of Italy, we learned. They had been caught hiding in a ditch. Unfortunately, it being winter, the shrubs lining the ditch were without leaves. They had been having their lunch, when the Austrian border patrol spotted them. At this revelation, Gerhard, sitting next to them, looked over at Irmgard, who nodded, as if to say, "See, I was right." Why were they hiding, and why so close to the border, in daylight, he wondered. Oh, no, they were not so close, they assured him. They had been up a hill waiting for the dark, so they could cross over into Italy. They had smuggled black coffee and tobacco into Austria and sold it on the black market. At this, Irmgard nudged the two sitting next to her, whispering, "hence the loose pants and jackets." The patrol had found all their good money; money paid in old silver and gold coins, which they had hidden in their shoes. Puka made one of his high whistles, while Hedy remarked with a short laugh: "They must have been happy!"

The object of Irmgard's initial repugnance soon proved itself but a prelude to what was to come. In the ensuing hour or two the new boarders kept taking urgent turns going to the latrine. In no time, and without needed prompting, Puka had the window pushed wide open, while we sisters defensively held our coat collars over our nose and mouth. As dusk settled, the trips to the latrine ceased and the two men, looking weak and drained, fell silent and, before long, fell asleep. Icy air was now sweeping through the open window, which even Gerhard felt no inclination to close. Instead, he stuck his face to the bars and called,

"Mr. Warden, Mr. Warden! Room number eleven, please!"

Mr. Warden didn't come running, of course, but took his time. Nor did he need to have explained to him the reason for the call. *"Halunken, Verfressene,"*—*Hooligans, gluttons,* he said with a voice and glance full of disdain at the two sleeping mates, while looking at the five of us for the first time with something like empathy and respect.

"You two!" he signaled, nodding toward Gerhard and Puka, who together fetched the bucket from the latrine and followed the warden.

Later that evening, did the warden come with a boiled potato, or a quarter of a steamed cabbage head, or a bowl of fish soup? If he did, I'm sure our brothers got to eat double portions, as the two Italians would, for the start at least, and in the light of their condition, have declined such fare. If, on the other hand, the warden happened to skip the evening meal because he had given us something at noon, this being Sunday, we sisters would, for once, not have missed it too much. The icy chill coming through the open window drove us under the blankets where we all too eagerly gave ourselves over to sleep.

12

OF TIME, HUNGER, AND OTHER THINGS

On the eve of our ninth prison day at Bruck an der Leitha—days that felt like months—the warden informed us that the following morning we would be transported to Vienna. When the time came, we eagerly climbed into the open back of the truck, where we sat on the floor close together to shield ourselves from the sub-freezing winter morning air. Despite the gray, sunless sky and cruel, icy wind that lashed our faces, half-freezing them, affecting our speech and smiles, we were hopeful and of good cheer. For, whether we had been told or had ourselves construed it, being taken to Vienna indicated that we would be taken before the appropriate authorities, who had already granted us Austrian asylum, or would upon hearing us.

To us, our transportation to Vienna signaled being soon set free; our having at long last arrived at our goal. The goal we had never lost sight of; that we carried in our hearts like a sacred grail, challenging us to risk and endure until we repossessed our freedom.

How stunned and thunderstruck we were, when after passing through various streets in Vienna, the truck stopped—not in front of a court or police headquarters, but in front of a long, gray building; stories high, with an iron gate, above which a sign read:

ROSSAUER LÄNDE GEFÄNGNIS
Verbesseungsanstalt

ROSSAUER STATE PRISON
Correctional Institution

Following the truck driver's urgings and beckoning arm gestures, *"Kommt! kommt!"—Come! come!* we climbed out. Speechless, as when we first stood in front of the fortress in Oradea Mare, so we now stood on the sidewalk—our eyes moving from the inscription to the driver, as if not comprehending. It was déjà vu.

Entering the gate that a prison guard unlocked, we walked like sentenced cattle through the empty, stone-paved courtyard. We were walking toward a multi-level blackish building with a bare façade, studded with iron-barred windows. Following a brief protocol and taking of fingerprints inside a large, heated room, a woman warden and a male warden stepped forward to take us to our respective cells. Too stunned to speak or cry, we sisters and brothers only looked at each other for a goodbye as we were led to our cells in different directions.

Once we were led first into a brightly-lit room, a gruff female warden posed the question of personal belongings. They would be taken and kept in a bag for safekeeping. Irmgard pulled the little journal and pencil from her coat pocket. *"Klumpert,"*—*Junk,* the coarse, loud-voiced warden announced as she threw the journal into the bag. Then we sisters were inspected for lice, with a steady stream of caustic remarks coming our way. Appraised as qualifying for treatment, our heads were unceremoniously doused with a strong and smelly solution. Humiliated, and with burning scalps and stinging eyes, the three of us walked up several flights of cement stairs and through an iron gate that the warden unlocked, and then clanked shut behind us. Then, a short corridor; the warden unlocking a door; and the eyes of some two dozen faces turned toward us as we stepped through the doorway.

"Wievel Uhr ist's?"—*What time is it?* a chorus of hopeful, eager voices greeted us.

"Neun,"—N*ine,* we answered.

"Erst?"—*Only?* came the swell of disappointed voices, followed by a fading, lamenting

"Oh . . ."

Startled at the time by this surreal greeting, we soon came to know that hunger and stagnant time were its origin. Hunger that loomed so large that time seemed to stand still; the time between a cup of coffee at seven or eight in the morning till a meager bowl of soup at noon seemed endless.

It was December 15 when we were placed behind locked gates and bars at the *Rossauer Lände prison* in Vienna. The cell in which we were to spend our daytimes had three long tables with backless benches on either side. Two chairs, and perhaps a small table, stood near the corner by one of the two windows. They were always occupied by the oldest woman and the youngest girl of the group. There were radiators under the windows, but they gave out no heat. Instead, the thick brick and plaster walls and the concrete floor exuded chill, as did the two large, barred windows without shades or shutters. Notwithstanding the free flow of chill coming through these windows, they were invaluable to us. True, they showed us an unredeemable stark, gray wall, but above and beyond that wall, they captured a broad patch of sky and with it the reminder of freedom of the large world, shrunk to non-existence inside. And although it appeared all cut-up by the bars, our eyes, accustomed to seeing it in its infinite aspect, were able to patch the pieces unnoticeably into a whole. Besides affording us three a vista onto both our hope and sorrow, they in time came to be also our timepieces, allowing us to read or gauge the approximate time of day from the progression and nuance of the entering light and dark.

The definite time-telling signals around which all our thinking and waiting revolved more and more intensely, were, of course, the three events of the day, regulated by the exact mechanism of the clock to which only the prison management had access. Any inmate who may have arrived at the gate of *the Rossauer Lände Gefängnis* with a wrist watch which, as by a miracle, hadn't been confiscated by Russian occupying forces or been pawned for more urgently-needed food or wood, naturally was obliged to surrender it for safekeeping. The three reliable daily time indicators between which we conducted our time readings were announced to us by loud, shrill, electrical bells at six o'clock in the morning; by the sound of rolling wheels and vibrating metal at noon, and again at five o'clock in the early evening. For the latter two, we spent hours waiting; hours of intense and desperate longing.

The shrill, persistent ringing at 6:00 a.m., accompanied by a flood of penetrating white light signaled the commencement of the institutionalized day: rising, folding the blanket, going to the large, cold, communal bathroom directly adjoining the huge sleeping hall, washing hands and face under running cold water. Then, walking in groups down two or three corridors, past a portable service station for the allotted mug of black, ersatz coffee; and into the half-dark day cell, lit by a single low-voltage bulb hanging from the ceiling on a long cord. Each woman sitting down at the same table and on the same spot on the bench—some gulping down the warm brew hungrily, others sipping it drop by drop—hoping against hope that time might contract to the approaching sound of rolling wheels and vibrating, clanking metal coming down the corridor and stopping near the cell door, announcing that it was noon, and food was coming. As the ears of all twenty-four women had been fixed on that sound—awaiting it and craving it for hours, so like a congregation at the priest's sign of invocation—all twenty-four women rose in unison to their feet at the sound of the key turning in the cell door.

And there was a repeat of the same ritual five hours later, when daylight had faded from the cell and the bulb suspended from the ceiling on a long, thin cord lit up the room as at a wake.

Did we get our daily piece of bread at noon, or was it given to us at night along with the bowl of soup; a little thicker than the one at noon? It will have been at noon, for I see daylight in the cell when, back at our tables and on our benches, we sat eating our bowl of thin soup and a piece of bread: first the soup, then the bread; drawing out the sensation of eating; of food.

I see us, twenty-four women, standing in line and around the serving station, everyone's eyes hungrily and woefully measuring one slice of bread against the others, each hoping that when her turn came, one of the thicker-appearing slices would fall to her lot. The old woman from the chair in the corner could often be heard begging in her Viennese folk-dialect: *"Bitt'schen, ach bitt'schen, geben's mir des Scherzl, bin a alt Frau und schwoch"*—*Please, oh please, give me the heel, am an old woman and weak*. Often she would get it, as might some other women who asked for it. We all could see that the end piece appeared to be the largest piece, but not all could bring themselves to ask for it, knowing that everyone longed to have it. I would eat my piece of bread slowly and mindfully, prolonging its taste and volume to the longest possible. Looking up one day, I saw several pairs of hungry eyes, including Irmgard's reproachful look fixed on the bread in my hand, theirs long gone. After that I kept my hand with the piece of bread in my lap, breaking off little chunks and eating them inconspicuously.

At the turning of the key, one hour after evening soup,

we would rise from our benches and walk in line, two by two, down corridors to the sleeping hall; adjoining the bathroom with some eighteen sinks on one wall and a lesser number of showers on the opposite wall. The latter were not for use. We sisters didn't stop here, but went straight to the sleeping hall and lay down in the same row and on the same spot of the long sleeping plank as on our first night here. We wanted to ensure that the three of us could lie next to each other and that we'd be returning to the same blankets, as repellent as they were.

It was freezing cold in here. Through large, open windows, subfreezing breezes swept all night over the heads and bodies of the sleepers. Lying on our sides, hugging close to each other allowed us, with some ingenuity, to extend our three narrow blankets; providing two layers for each. (Any turning had to be done in unison.) The coarse blankets (so repulsive, one didn't want to touch them) we pulled over our heads and tucked in at the sides in order to trap and conserve body heat, and mitigate the onslaught of the brutal cold from the outside.

How we craved sleep, refuge from consciousness, deliverance from discomfort, sorrow; all. But sleep was hard to come by. Gnawing hunger, aching, unpadded bones against unpadded wooden planks, trembling bodies and chattering teeth were keeping us awake for hours—until the little bit of shared body heat and exhaustion finally gave way to merciful sleep. Seldom, if ever, was our sleep undisturbed. There was no night when one of us sisters or someone in the sleeping hall didn't start up with nightmares or, as frequently happened, by the wailing, shrill sound of approaching sirens, followed by screeching wheels, brazen light lighting up the sleeping hall, and honking of horns coming from the prison courtyard through the open windows. A moment of silence—then male voices shouting orders, a buzz of high-pitched young female voices and before long, a rush of clicking high heels in the corridors coming closer; giggles, laughter—and suddenly, silence. The second time we were awakened by this theater of sounds, light and voices, Irmgard whispered to the woman closest to her to ask what was going on.

"*Ach, Freudenmädchen*"—*Joy girls*; they round them up and deliver them here." Irmgard had to define "*Freudenmädchen*" to me. I learned that the word signified prostitute.

In time we learned from conversations over the tables in the day cell that these nightly activities, extending sometimes into the early morning hours, were the result of round-ups by the local Austrian and American allied forces stationed in Vienna that conducted raids on bars, clubs and other such locales where occupying forces hung out and were consequently visited by local prostitutes, as well as by girls and young women—not necessarily all Viennese or Austrian. The prevailing grimness of post-war times—starvation, food, fuel and housing shortages, depletion of the native male population, joblessness and demoralization—drove both fun-seeking and destitute females to these spots. Chocolate bars, nylon stockings, cigarettes and other treats could easily be exchanged on the black market for money, food, wood and other necessities. With this input, my two older sisters concluded from some rather open comments by the parties in question that at least two, but perhaps three of the young and more lighthearted women in our day cell had come to Rossauer Lände Gefängnis by way of these round-ups. One of them was a non-Austrian. Owing to their unprofessional (i.e. unregistered) status, they were placed not with prostitutes but with women inmates like us, held for other reasons.

I do not remember if I actually understood all these references at the time. But I do remember the liveliest and most expressive one of these "lighthearted" young women. She had ash-blond hair and was perhaps nineteen years old.

Among the other inmates who sat with us on the benches, sometimes exchanging a few words with each other and occasionally directing some questions at Irmgard as well as answering those she asked, three women were sitting in the *Rossauer Lände Gefängnis* for the same reasons we were. They were ethnic Germans from one of the former Austro-Hungarian regions who had fled to Austria from persecution, then were caught and placed in prison for lack of a passport and permit.

More distinct than these in my memory is the old woman who always sat apart in the corner with the youngest girl by her side. She was homeless. She had been bombed out as well as widowed in one of the air raids on Vienna, and was incarcerated because she was found sleeping on park benches at night. Sleeping on park benches was unlawful. This was her third stay at *Rossauer Lände Gefängnis*, each time for the same reason. Irmgard, more skeptical than I, suspected that in winter she preferred her prison stay to her park benches in freezing temperatures. I don't remember if I ever knew why the young, quiet girl was serving a sentence. Not older than eleven or twelve, wearing a short winter coat and her light brown hair in shoulder-length braids, she always sat, walked, and slept at the side of the old woman. They were not related. Perhaps she too had become homeless in an air raid and also orphaned. Perhaps they had met in one of Vienna's many lovely parks, and having nowhere to go and no one to go to, they bonded and became like grandmother and granddaughter, keeping each other company and making one another feel that they were safer and happier for not being alone. If this was their story, they must, in a way, have been glad to be spending the winter months within the walls of the *Rossauer* prison.

Judging by this prison, as the one in Bruck and der Leitha, the Austrian post-war prison population included a diverse and motley group representing various ethnicities, nations, and elements of society whose historical lives and life paths had been written by the far-reaching effects of the War. How many, one wonders, would in time find their way back to normalcy, to a place in society, to the dignities and fulfillments of a life?

The young, light-hearted woman, bound to be remembered by everyone, was sitting opposite me at the table across from ours. She seemed uninhibited, untroubled and carefree, and, as Irmgard judged, enormously bored. Unlike the rest of us, she enjoyed the occasional privilege of access to one of her personal belongings. It was a cosmetic box, the first I had ever laid my eyes on. Attached to the inside of the lid was a good-sized mirror. One by one she'd lift from her treasure chest little tubes, boxes, pencils and brushes that she would set out on the table in purposeful sequence. Except for the other two, not-too-serious young women, who exchanged observations with her on the subject at hand, the rest of us watched her in silence, like an audience before a stage. The drama performed here was a cunning scheme of enhancement and transformation, engendered by a deft hand and trained, knowing eye. Her face set and examined in the mirror from various angles, she'd look up and around as if to signal the time for applause.

"There, one's right away looking and feeling better. Without it, everything is so deadly boring,"—*zum Sterben fad*, she announced, looking picked-up and satisfied. But the young cellmate's versatility and talent was not limited to the art of applying makeup. She could project different personas in face, movement, and posture; ranging from the charming, innocent *"Süsse Wiener Mädl"—the sweet, Viennese girl* to the dark "femme fatal" of a Lulu.

Seeing her one afternoon standing by the window, gesticulating animatedly I asked Irmgard what she was doing—acting as if she was talking to someone?

"She is flirting; having a rendezvous with a man behind one of those barred windows."

"So they know each other?"

"Just from standing by their cell windows and exchanging sign language through the bars," Irmgard answered.

On a similar occasion somewhat later, Irmgard turned to Hedy and me and observed that she, the flirting young woman, was hoping that the man would meet her at the chapel service on Christmas Day, adding, "She is already counting the days." Touching on these rendezvous interludes in conversation decades later, Irmgard characterized them summarily as "a romance in prison, born of isolation and boredom, and ignited by the spirit of adventure."

Our thoughts often went to our brothers, wondering what had happened to them and how they were doing. We hadn't seen, heard from, or learned anything about them, which often made us feel anxious and sad. Inspired by the blonde's window outreach, and on the chance that our brothers might have been placed in one of the other three buildings facing the large, rectangular, barren courtyard paved in cobblestones, my eyes now began to scale the walls and endless rows of windows across from us. At first, I did so from my bench seat. The view from here was, of course, limited—and as it yielded no results, I decided to take up my search from the windows. First, though, I let it be known that my purpose and hope was to possibly spot our brothers, who might be searching for the sight of us from their windows. After several attempts at detecting a face or figure behind the bars in the numberless windows, most too distant to yield even the outline of a person, I gave up searching. We would have to wait for the promise of Christmas Day.

As in Oradea Mare, so here in Vienna, I was selected to clean municipal offices. Not that I was the sturdiest—far from it—but my long, thick brown braids and large brown eyes, as well as my quietness, must have fit our warden's idea of innocence.

Prisoners, guilty and non-guilty alike, could not question or object to orders. Thus, when our warden appeared in the doorway one morning and pointed to me, announcing that starting today, I'd be working in the municipal offices, I turned to my sisters, kissed them, and followed her. Naturally, I felt apprehensive, as did my sisters, who had reached for my hands and tightly squeezed them. In the prison office where we had been fingerprinted, I was instructed about the scope of my duties and about what was off limits. I was to sweep and if necessary, mop the office floors, empty wastebaskets, dust, and carry out other jobs that might be requested. I was not to attempt to engage the staff in conversation, and I was not to flirt, pry, or steal. I should do my work properly (*"anständig"*), and keep the appropriate distance. A maintenance officer assigned to be my guard would be bringing me, and returning me afterward.

Although I felt offended by this litany of do's and

don'ts I took everything silently and when asked if I understood, I answered with a brief *"ja."* Nor did I complain that every morning before leaving the prison, my guard would have me follow him with two large, empty buckets down a steep flight of stairs into a dimly-lit cellar filled with mounds of coal where, handed a shovel, I would fill up the buckets and then stagger with them up the stairs, while he followed behind me empty-handed.

I remember feeling taken aback at the man's callousness. I suspected that the lugging of coal was more likely his job assignment. It surprised me, somehow, not to be met with greater empathy and solidarity by someone in a humble position himself, who would have known from his own experience the bitterness of powerlessness.

"Unverschämt!"—*How shameful!* Hedy and Irmgard declared in unison when I told them of the hauling the coal after my first prison outing. In the end, however, the man showed himself to be more sensitive. After he had been out with an illness for a couple of days, he seemed to have softened. He now would pick up one of the full buckets and carry it up the cellar stairs, explaining, "It must be quite heavy for you; after all you aren't exactly the strongest. What are you, thirteen, fourteen? You can't be more than that!" I didn't volunteer an answer, telling him, as I had told the kind

farmer woman in Romania, that I was fifteen.

Leaving the *Rossauer Lände Gefängnis* from a side gate, we would then turn right onto the boulevard and walk several blocks to a busy intersection. The municipal building was situated diagonally opposite of where we'd stand waiting for traffic to ease so we could safely cross to the other side. The building had something welcoming about it, perhaps because it wasn't as dark and tall as most buildings along the boulevard. But mainly, it was, I believe, the wide entrance. A few steps leading up to the generous platform could be ascended from the various points of a broad angle. This, and the glass doors set into wooden frames, suggested accessibility and easy flow between the inside and the outside. Yet, each time we approached the corner, I could feel apprehension rising, despite the promising comfort of hours spent in the warm, well-lit rooms.

Arriving at the offices on the second morning, a couple of male clerks greeted me with *"Guten Morgen!"* The next day, a young woman with shoulder-length blond hair looked up from her desk and said, smiling, *"Guten Morgen, Dora!"* Within the same hour, an older, well-dressed woman politely asked me to take special care with the stack of printed pages that she wanted moved from her desk.

It had been so long since I had been acknowledged in this way. The unexpected civil and friendly tone surprised me. As a declared enemy, prisoner, and refugee I had obviously come to feel not entitled, if not undeserving of such common human courtesy; particularly from persons of authority. And while a part of me was moved to childlike gratitude and joy, another part wept.

At noon of the third day, an office supervisor informed me that lunch was being served in the cafeteria below and that he, like the staff, was on his way to have lunch there. I, too, should come to the cafeteria and eat. Whether in reaction to my astonishment at this unexpected invitation, or because I may have said *"Ich darf nicht"*—*I'm not allowed to*, or because I had indicated in my anxiousness that I had no money to buy myself lunch, he assured me that no one would object to my coming to the cafeteria and that I didn't need any money, as my work here entitled me to a free lunch. With all my hesitations thus refuted, I thanked him. At the door leading down to the cafeteria he looked back and, pointing to the descending staircase called *"Also gut, da unten, ja?"*—*Ok, then, down here, yes?*

I didn't follow him at once. I would have infinitely preferred not to go. My apprehension and shyness were greater than my hunger. How could I intrude into this circle of normal, well-dressed, self-confident, happy people? But the office supervisor had been nice to me and had obviously meant well. I had thanked him, which he took as "yes". I walked toward the door;

stood by the staircase. The clamor of voices from down below carried up the stairwell. It frightened me, but I couldn't turn back—I had to go down.

Slowly, I descended, wishing for the stairs to never end. The voices intermingled with laughter were getting louder as I was getting closer. I was almost at the foot of the staircase. The door to the cafeteria was wide open, filled with women and men seated at tables, talking and laughing. Some faces were turned toward me, questioning or perhaps surprised, but not unkind. Standing in the tiny corridor at the foot of the stairs, a few feet away from the threshold of the cafeteria, I furtively glanced to my left, hoping to spot a door through which I might escape. But there was only a door to the cafeteria kitchen and another large door with a bar across it.

Feeling like an intruder, and aware that my shoes were torn and dirty, my stockings full of runs and holes, my dress and coat rumpled, my hair unwashed, my fingernails blackened with coal dust, I once again felt diminished and deeply humiliated. But as retreat upstairs seemed impossible, I entered.

The room was crowded and warm, filled with the odor of hot food, cigarette smoke, and the hum of voices. Slowly, I wound my way between the occupied round tables as if looking for an empty chair. Startled, some of the diners looked up questioningly, while others bent down to their plates or turned to a neighbor. Had one of those southeastern *"Volksdeutsche"*—war refugees, parked on their bundles on the streets of the city's subway and train stations, somehow lost her way into their midst? I continued moving, passing up an occasional empty chair—for how would I have the audacity, I thought, to seat myself amongst these clean, cheerful people so vivaciously engaged in conversation and laughter? Somehow, I made my way to the now-empty tables in the back. Some of the cafeteria help—women standing behind their steamer trays—were looking expectantly at me, taking me for a straggling customer. An older, motherly-looking one with a flushed, plump face nodded more than once invitingly. Compelled, I got up, walked into their area, took a plate and passed the trays; looking at the contents of each as if to decide which held the greatest appeal to me, only to return to the table in back with a still-empty plate.

The last diners were leaving and the younger women behind the steam tables were abandoning their posts with plates of food for their own lunch. The older, motherly woman, however, had stayed behind. She was looking over. Her smile and expression told me that she understood what was holding me back. *"Na komm, da is noch Essen!"*—*Come, there's still some food,* she encouraged me, addressing me with the familiar "du". *"Komm nur, s'wird dir gut tun, s'warme Essen!"*—*Just come, the warm food will do you good*, she encouraged me a second time. Pointing to a tray to her left, she tried to coax me once more: "Look at this here, the cheese noodles with the breadcrumbs, you're sure to like this." I got up and walked toward the serving area. But I didn't go in. I couldn't. Inside, I was frozen with fear and crying with sorrow. I thanked her, walked out of the cafeteria and up the stairs.

Having been exiled too early and too long from society and deprived too long of my natural rights and claims, I was not able to suddenly take up my place with ease and matter-of-factness in a group of free persons. I had become a stranger to normal, every-day life. And though I was shy and frightened, there was still pride in me.

Much like a dog of good breeding who's fallen on ill luck, losing his home and master, and becoming subject to intimidation and mistreatment, who may slowly, reticently approach a person or table only to turn and run when a hand reaches out to him, spurning the food offered him, so I had come and left the cafeteria without having sat down with others or taking the food offered to me.

For reasons I no longer remember, Irmgard once or twice came to substitute for me at the municipal offices.

What I do remember, however, was the excitement reflected in her face after her first prison outing. She spoke of the expansive grandeur of the boulevard with its impressive buildings and trees; its vibrancy. "What a beautiful city Vienna is, a grand metropolis," she exclaimed to Hedy and me; "and we're sitting here," she groaned, gesturing with her head toward the cell with hungry women huddled around the tables. And a gray curtain of frustration and hopelessness drew once again over her face.

In Gerhard's absence, my older sister was spared the teasing and grins in response to her passion for culture. I, on the other hand, registered how different her experience was from mine, even though, on returning from my first outing, I, too, had spoken to my sisters about the imposing, bustling scenes on the tree-lined boulevard. Yet, fear and apprehension had not colored her experience and conduct as they had mine. But Irmgard was older, more assertive and inquisitive by nature, whereas I was timid and dreamy as if hovering between two worlds.

Upon our incarceration at *Rossauer Lände Gefängnis,* Irmgard had almost immediately begun to inquire about legal hearings and appeals. But neither our cellmates nor our warden were able to furnish her with any useful information.

"You're just gonna have to wait your turn" the warden had responded nonchalantly in Viennese dialect. The three ethnic German women, who were detained in prison for the same reason as we, were unaware of any legal procedure having been filed on their behalf; though they had already spent two months in prison. In other words, there appeared to be no system in place for initiating a hearing, no established schedule for hearings, no recourse for legal advice and representation. As Irmgard would later note, "This was profoundly demoralizing, designed, as it were, to overwhelm one with a sense of helplessness. In this state of limbo where every option and move felt impeded, we came to feel more and more forgotten."

Having learned from another warden that we were entitled to send a card to a contact person in Vienna, Irmgard at once dispatched a note to a colleague and friend of our father's, Pastor Ferdinand Mayr. In lieu of an address, she mailed it to the Methodist Church, Vienna, Austria. Apprising him of our situation, she appealed for his help to bring about our release. The thought that someone on the outside knew of us, and would take steps on our behalf, raised our spirits and hope. We expected to hear back from Herr Mayr quickly. However, when days passed without getting word from him, and there was still no tangible sign of a process having been set into motion for our release, our optimism began to dampen again. Christmas was not far off and our cherished hope that we would spend Christmas in freedom was slowly fading.

Given the season, our thoughts turned to the rest of the family and memories of the joy and warmth of rooms filled with Christmas celebration; recollections evoking painful longings, worry, and fear for our loved ones as well as the bitterness of feeling excluded. In the dayroom, the growing silence and sadness that we shared became palpable.

A bleak winter sky hung as an opaque curtain outside the windows, obscuring even the opposite gray prison wall with its many barred windows. Soon dusk would fill the room prematurely. I was sitting between my two sisters, as usual. They, like the rest of us, sat as if sunk into themselves. We had been like that for some time, when something made me look up at Irmgard. Her face, which had come to look sad and discouraged, was now radiant and calm, glowing with deep joy and peace. She turned and, seeing my questioning gaze, nodded, "It's all right," and sighing deeply, repeated, "Everything is all right." Taking my hand into her strong, warm clasp and nodding her head toward the room, she explained, "I had been thinking about all this... and then I was thinking of God... and how this could be... and then I saw an incredible light and felt an infinite joyful peace... and I knew it was all right."

It is one thing to uphold one's faith, the faith of one's mother and father, and to keep in one's heart the name of God, and it was quite another thing to be able to say and feel that all this was all right. Yet, something dimly resonated within me. As if dropping into a dark well where, bouncing against narrow walls, her words set off echoes the way ringing chimes reverberate in towers before their sound is carried into the open.

For a moment, I stood in the fortress courtyard in Oradea Mare, saw and felt the lightness, the infinite tenderness as of a young bird's feather. Again, I saw my father's face as he last spoke to me with his hand on my shoulder: "Remember Dora, my child, God meets us on many different paths. This may be the one on which he'll meet you." Warm tears were rolling down my face. I didn't stop or wipe them away with my coat sleeve. Feeling Hedy's hand on my arm, I turned to her: "I was remembering Tata there on the corner when the three of us were taken away to the vineyard labor camp." Recalling, Hedy nodded, and took my hand. Her gaze was so still with resignation, turned as to a place far away.

13

NOT FORGOTTEN

December 24th had arrived. We anticipated with dread Christmas Eve. Would it come upon us hurdling us into a downward descent? As the afternoon light faded into winter dusk, the room was wrapped in hushed silence. More and more heads were turned toward the windows as if expecting to see the night sky suddenly alight with a large Christmas tree with white burning candles; a large shimmering star; or the tall lit spire of the Stephansdom, rising like a phoenix from the war rubbles. Perhaps the church bells might ring, proclaiming Christmas tidings—penetrating the dense plaster of the prison walls, chiming to the excluded and forgotten ones imprisoned within.

A woman at the table in front of us reached under her coat and pulled out a candle and matches, lifting them up like a host for everyone to see. We gasped. How did she get hold of them? We all had been stripped of our personal belongings, and the possession of contraband such as matches was strictly forbidden. But, it was Christmas Eve: Perhaps someone's heart had been moved, and a warden was averting her eyes from this. We pushed the three tables together and placed the six benches around them. "Come, you too," the woman with the candle called, and the old woman and girl left their corner and sat down with us. The woman now lit the candle. Another switched off the meager light bulb hanging from the ceiling. All twenty-four women and girls sat in silence looking into the flickering light of the single candle; traveling to other times and places. Their bodies seemed to feel less cold.

Someone said, "You sisters, come, sing a Christmas song. You must know a lot of them."

"Yes, sing one," urged several more.

The three of us began to sing with halting voices:

> *"Oh du fröhliche,*
> *Oh du selige,*
> *Gnade bringende Weihnachtszeit. . ."*

. . . the song our family always sang, to open our Christmas Eve celebration. When we sang:

> *"Stille Nacht, Heilige Nacht. . ."*—Silent
> Night, Holy Night. . .

... other voices joined in the second stanza, rising to a chorus of all our voices in the third.

The sound of a key turning in the door lock abruptly brought the singing to a halt. The warden stood on the threshold. What would happen? Had she suspected something? Would she reprimand us for burning a candle or for singing so loudly? She did neither. Instead, she called out:

"*Irmgard Drumm, kommen's, jemand is hier für Sie!*"— *Irmgard Drumm, come out, someone is here to see you*! Astonished, Irmgard's face lit up with excitement and hope. Rising, she whispered to Hedy and me:

"You know, of course, that it is for all of us."

Who might this be? Who had come on Christmas Eve to see us at the *Rossauer Lände Gefängnis*? Hedy and I wondered. It must be Herr Mayr, we concluded, for he alone could know we were here. Under the heavy blanket of my great weariness, I could feel hope gently stirring. Someone on the outside knew of us; someone in this large, unfamiliar city remembered us and had come to this prison to see us. Hedy was holding my hand tightly, as if to ensure that this would not turn out to be a mirage like the phantom field hut on that first night of our flight. Her clasp was strong and soft at once, and more giving and tender than she could be with words.

When Irmgard returned, carrying a large, flat, white box in her hands, she was struggling to contain her emotions and tears. Never wanting to be seen crying, she also forbade herself from displaying her joy too freely out of consideration for the feelings of the women, whom no one had called on this evening.

"It was family friends who learned of our stay here," she explained. Removing the lid from the white box, she announced:

"There are enough Christmas cookies for each person to have two, and some for our brothers here." After we had chosen ours, the box of assorted cookies was passed around from hand-to-hand with many "Ah!" and "Danke schön!"—*Thank you.*

I moved over to let Irmgard take the middle seat. Unable to contain ourselves any longer, Hedy and I lowered our voices:

"Who was it?"

"Frau Zoffmann and Else."

"Frau Zoffmann and Else are in Vienna? How do they know we are here?" Hedy and I exclaimed.

"Through Herr Mayr," Irmgard retorted and, anticipating our next question, she proceeded to give us some more background.

Frau Zoffmann and Else, along with Inge and Frau Zoffmann's mother had been living in Vienna ever since they fled there from camp. They contacted Herr Mayr at the Methodist Church soon after they got there, figuring that he would know our father. And from them, he learned the whole story of what had happened to us and the other ethnic Germans across Yugoslavia. So when he received Irmgard's card, he at once appealed to the authorities for our release and residence permit, and notified the Zoffmanns of our whereabouts.

"Oh, yes," Irmgard remembered, "greetings from the Zoffmann's and Herr Mayr. They said to not give up hope." With these greetings from our Christmas Eve visitors, the tension that had built inside Irmgard from the enormous uplift of the unexpected reunion with the Zoffmanns and the good news, finally gave way to tears.

I imagine that Hedy and I joined her in weeping tears of gratitude and hope; tears for our loved ones and for the pain and suffering in the world.

Our friendship with the Zoffmanns stemmed from our internment camp days. They were amongst the seventy of us; women and girls who had been moved from the central internment camp in Vršac to the labor camp on the outskirts of town; rented out to do vineyard work. Our youngest sister, Claudia, had originally been a classmate of and friends with Frau Zoffmann's youngest daughter, Inge. Claudi, as we called her, would also frequently visit Inge at her home as well as occasionally spend summer vacation days at the family's beautiful villa, located on a hillside outside of town.

The Zoffmanns were wealthy wine growers and merchants and employed many hands. They were natives of Vršac and its ethnic German community and, like the majority of them, Roman Catholic. We had limited contact with them, as our family was none of these. We were newcomers—a protestant minister's family who lacked wealth, and did not cultivate specifically ethnic German ties. Our parents insisted that we children attend Serbian primary and secondary schools until the German occupation, when all ethnic German children were mandated to attend German schools. In the internment camp we had come to know them more closely. Frau Zoffmann had a serious heart condition. With the help of her elderly mother—of hardy farm stock and still strong—as well as their former Serbian manager who returned her past kindness with an underground supply of medicine, Frau Zoffmann managed to put in the same ten- or twelve-hour workday as all the others. She never complained, not even when they were now forced as prisoners, to tend their own confiscated vineyards in sight of their stately villa—which strangers from the Communist elite now occupied, lunching and tanning on the wide terraces.

The Zoffmanns had escaped several months before us. Irmgard would tell me years later that Frau

Zoffmann had approached her about our fleeing with them. She had offered to pay the fee charged by the underground guides for us. But Irmgard had declined her offer because we couldn't bring ourselves to leave our mother and two youngest siblings behind, knowing their whereabouts. Frau Zoffmann had tried to sway Irmgard, entreating her to think of our future. When it became clear that Irmgard wouldn't be swayed, Frau Zoffmann wept at the prospect of leaving us behind. She did, however, leave our brother, Gerhard, information about the two underground guides who had taken the Zoffmann family, and who would later take us to the Romanian border. This, too, I learned many years later. Secrets were kept secret, even from closest of kin, so as not to put others unnecessarily at risk in the event of interrogation.

When I wondered how the Zoffmanns, who had lost everything—as we all had—could have come up with so much money (no less than 7,000 dinars for themselves and us), Irmgard divulged their secret: "They had prepared for eventualities," she said. As the German army was retreating and the Russian army advanced at their heels, the Zoffmanns switched buttons on their coats and sweaters with new fabric ones. Under the fabric cover of each button were valuable gold coins. A trusted seamstress had crafted this disguise; cleverer and safer than Gerhard's scheme with the silver ducats.

The Winds of Fortress Kula

The day before Christmas Eve, a warden had informed Irmgard of Chapel Services being held on Christmas Day, asking if we wished to go. Irmgard had at once said, "Yes"—and in the next breath, she inquired if our brothers would be attending. The warden didn't know, since the male section of the prison lay outside her preview. As it turned out, only three women from our cell were allowed to attend the Christmas Service along with us. The ash-blonde was not amongst those selected. This proved a real disappointment to her, causing her usual upbeat spirit to be greatly dampened. I was surprised and felt badly for her and for the others who weren't given this opportunity. It struck me as contradictory that the officials wouldn't be inviting those who were supposedly here to be "reformed."

Chancing many years later on the subject of the ash-blonde's disappointment, Irmgard recalled that her dejection had less to do with being barred from the Christmas Service, than with the loss of her much-desired chance to rendezvous with that male prisoner whom she had spotted one day, standing at his cell window in a building across from ours.

"Do you remember how she'd stand by the window and flirt with him?" Irmgard asked.

"Yes, I do. But they must have barely been able to see each other." I now recalled the scenario staged at the left window of our day cell at a favorable afternoon hour each day to maximize visibility. Young, lighthearted, bored and undeterred by the bars and gaping distance between the opposing windows and the plunging drop to the cobblestone pavement below, a drama of flirtation and communication, deftly choreographed by means of mime and sign language with outstretched arms through the bars of the windows, unfolded.

Eagerly, with the impulse of both heart and spirit, we anticipated the Chapel Service. We so much wanted to see our brothers and share the good news with them. And we longed to be uplifted by the message of Christmas.

As we entered the chapel, our brothers were already sitting on the right side of the aisle designated for male inmates. Our eyes met immediately. It struck me that the light had now greatly dimmed in their sunken eyes. I wanted to run over and put my arms around their frail shoulders and hold them, but prison protocol forbade the crossing of lines.

We exchanged smiles. Their smiles were now thin lines on their pale, gaunt faces. We went and sat in a pew on the left side of the aisle, a couple of rows from our brothers, from where we could look at each other without being too conspicuous.

When the chaplain entered from a side door of the nave and mounted the pulpit, signaling the commencement of the Service and with it, the closing of the chapel doors, there were seemingly more empty pews and seats than there were occupied. Why were so few attending from this large prison complex? Later, when the chords of the last hymnal were fading, Hedy whispered into my ear, alluding to those who had been excluded: "They didn't miss much, did they?"

As Irmgard would write later, "...with an explosive voice and disdainful expression, the chaplain projected a list of transgressions and sins upon us, following this with a call to search our consciences and souls, and repent." During much of the service, Hedy had sat with lowered eyes, her lips turning to a wry smile at particularly fiery charges. While Puka would steal glances from across the aisle at appropriate moments, Gerhard looked steadily at the speaker as if taking in every word. Was he weighing these words against what he had come to know in his heart and spirit? Did they move him to some resolve about how not to be? As our visibly disappointed and indignant sister Irmgard would later recall, "Why, he had talked as if we were all hardened criminals who had committed grave crimes against God, humanity, and our own souls." The Chaplain had left little room for the Christmas message of peace and love.

Filing out of our pews and milling toward the chapel door, we managed to have a quick exchange. Irmgard informed our brothers of the Zoffmanns' visit. At this news, their faces lit up. While she filled in Gerhard on further details, Puka lowered his voice to tell Hedy and me how the two of them were in a cell with regular criminals; "richtige Diebe"—*real thieves*, who, when delivered to their cell, had razorblades on them. Having stepped outside the chapel doors into a courtyard with some bare trees, our contact was cut off. The women were being lined up to the right; the men to the left. As we were escorted back to our cells, Irmgard turned to call out, *"Also bald!"*—*Soon, then!* to our brothers. Puka flashed us a victory sign in response.

Barely out of their earshot, we expressed our alarm over the changes our brothers had undergone since we had last seen them three weeks ago. Their coats now hung from them as if they belonged to men with frames two times larger. Having been with each other every day, we were not as aware of similar changes in our own appearance. In retrospect, I would realize that on that Christmas Day Gerhard already displayed signs of the illness that would take him to death's door, and from which he would recover as if by a miracle.

Upon our return, the women in our day room looked at us questioningly. Irmgard reported that the only uplifting thing in the service itself had been the music, specifically the solo piece sung by a young woman, a student at the Vienna Music Conservatory, to a piano accompaniment. Irmgard described her beautiful voice, and went on to tell how she had a standing performance engagement at one of Vienna's large churches. She had sung from Handel's *Messiah* which, following this service, she would also sing at that church. Ignoring the singer's credentials, the old woman turned from the window to remark: "Like the song of birds when I wake each morning in the park."

On a dark forenoon, shortly after Christmas, two women joined the twenty-four of us in the day room. They were not greeted with the question of what time it was. One glance and everyone knew that they, particularly one, had never been without comfort, luxury, or shelter. One was more elegant and beautiful, and visibly more privileged. Judging by the other's more modest appearance and demeanor, as well as by her continuous effort to comfort and encourage the distraught and crying lady, one surmised that she was the other's attendant.

They didn't sit down on the benches with us. They sat on chairs in the corner close to us.

We could overhear them: They spoke Serbian. Exchanging some words with them in their native language, Irmgard learned that they were from Belgrade, that they had been caught trying to enter Austria and were found to have large quantities of valuables on them. Irmgard guessed that they had probably carried forged IDs. Gazing at their footwear, she also guessed that they had crossed the border by automobile or train. Irmgard didn't learn their motives for escaping from their homeland, or whether the husband and son the lady had left behind intended to follow.

According to Irmgard, no one in the day room had been particularly moved by the lady's tears, complaints, and fears; her misfortunes seemed relatively small, both in time and extent. Recalling how the ladies had abstained from the bowl of soup and bread dished out to them, Irmgard observed that, obviously not hungry themselves, it had not occurred to them to take the food and offer it to others who were starving. Irmgard judged the two women as spoiled, self-absorbed and ignorant; particularly the more privileged one, who from all evidence had the exceptional means and connections to obtain nylon hose—a sensational new invention from America, obtainable only on the black market. I suspect Hedy would have agreed with Irmgard.

Two days after they had joined us, a warden took one step into the room, called the two Serbian women's names, and asked them to follow her. They got up from their chairs and left, and did not return again. The unaccustomed speed with which the authorities appeared to be attending to their case gave rise to speculation which, in the end, reminded each one of us even more sharply of our own languishing and helplessness. Between them, Irmgard and Hedy shared the opinion that at worst, the two ladies would be returned to their government.

While not disagreeing with my two elder sisters' appraisal, I nonetheless noted quietly how, for me, the appearance of the elegant lady from Belgrade had the effect of an elixir, lifting for the duration of its power, the numbing reality. My astonished eyes were feasting on this beauty and elegance, the exquisite richness and suppleness of fabrics. In the midst of such long, weary bleakness, her presence stirred buried joys and wonderment inside me; quickening life within me like a winter rose on the shaded hillside pushing through a blanket of snow.

Sometime between Christmas and the New Year, the three of us were summoned to the prison office. I remember us going down the stairs, full of anticipation. Halfway down, we met Gerhard and Puka. Joyfully, we embraced and began to speculate about what the summons might mean. It bode well, we thought. Puka mockingly suggested that perhaps we were finished here; reformed.

Stepping into a room, we ran with cries of surprise and joy into the open arms of Frau Zoffmann and Else. Then I noticed a gentleman standing at the side, quietly looking on. From photos I had seen of Father with his colleagues, I at once recognized the minister, Prediger Mayr. The sparkling blue eyes through the gold-rimmed lenses, the facial features and the short, slim figure in the dark coat were unmistakably his. We introduced ourselves and shook hands.

"I've taken all the legal steps for your release, but you need to be patient for a few more days," he told us.

Irmgard's lines, written within a few months of our release, resonate with the immediacy of the experience Herr Mayr's report had on us: "It was difficult to fully grasp and believe that it would actually still happen. Nonetheless, we returned to our cells with joyful hearts. And although it was still as cold in there, and although our hunger continued to grow into ever greater proportions, with our new hope, everything seemed more tolerable."

The New Year had passed. We hadn't received further word from Herrr Mayr, and there were no new signs of our release. And though it was not yet a week since our happy meeting with the Zoffmanns and Pastor

Mayr, time felt leaden and hope felt as tenuous as the balancing act of a tightrope walker.

Then one morning, a warden called us out and informed us that we were to shower and wash our hair. The warden did not take us to the large bathroom next to our sleeping hall. Instead, she led us down an unfamiliar corridor. With every turn of a corner and new brightly- or dimly-lit corridor, unease was rising inside us. Where was she taking us? Would we find our way out of this maze? The warden must have sensed our apprehension, for she tried to reassure us, telling us that the water would be warm.

The bathroom we entered was white and tiled as the other, but smaller. Along the left sidewall were some five or six showers stalls. After brief instructions, she placed three towels on a chair. She would be by in a while, she called over her shoulder before exiting.

We did not rush into the shower as one might expect, neither from joy over the promise of warm water, nor from the opportunity to cleanse ourselves of a layer of film from the months of living on the road as fugitives and in prison. Rather, we stood with coats and scarves still on, with hunched shoulders as if lost. Only when we heard the warden call out briskly, "Well, are you making out ok? It will be nice and warm in there," did we set about removing our clothes. Since we would be putting them back on, one by one, unwashed as they were, we carefully laid each on top of the other. Our clothes were layered in the same order as on the day we had fled from our labor internment camp.

I took off my knitted woolen gloves, both thumbs half worn through; my headscarf that I had worn constantly, almost as if it had become a layer of skin; and my indigo-blue winter coat—the first coat my mother had tailored for my maturing figure—with two front rows of buttons and side pockets which held my sole belongings: two large cotton handkerchiefs, gray from time and wear. Then followed a waist-length, knitted woolen sweater, and a knee-length woolen skirt with two kick-pleats. Underneath all this, a form-fitting dress with covered buttons down to the waist, round collar and side zipper. My brown, ankle-high lace shoes, their leather so scuffed, cracked, and dirty that one couldn't be certain about their color. Large holes were worn through the soles and the laces were torn and knotted, making them too short to lace to the top. Two pairs of long, thick, beige cotton stockings, with runs and holes worn through the knees and feet, and a set of underwear. The sweater, skirt, and dress—rather pretty and fashionable in design—had been smuggled into our labor camp by a family friend a few weeks before we escaped. They had been part of a CARE package sent through a Methodist Church in the U.S. to Father's parish and address.

In the mirrors above the washbasins across from the shower stalls we saw with shock the reflection of our naked bodies. We did not recognize them as ours. Bones were protruding everywhere. Our ribcages were visible, bellies sunken, breasts nearly gone. Our monthly cycles had come to a stop some time ago. Startled, we looked down at our own bodies as if at something alien. With pity we now glanced at each other's emaciated figures, exclaiming, "O, Hedy!" "O, Igat!" "O, Dori!"

For Irmgard, the warden's mention of showers on that January morning evoked yet another unsettling experience. As she would confide to me many years later, she was overcome by a profound and inexplicable sense of unease. She clearly remembered not wanting to enter the shower stall but felt compelled to do so when the warden returned and inquired how we were making out in there. Much later, when she read reports that substantiated occasional hushed rumors during the German occupation about the methods employed upon Nazi concentration camp victims, Irmgard understood what it was she had dreaded.

Strangely, we had not read our showering privileges as indicative of our imminent release. Laced with mystery and unease, it startled and perplexed rather than buoyed us. Or had we become so weary?

14

OUTSIDE THE PRISON GATES

Below her last entry in the palm-sized notebook, pre-dating our incarceration at the *Rossauer Lände Gefängnis* in Vienna, appears a new strong line. Underneath the line, in big dancing letters, the words:

"Drumm Mädel, kommt 'raus, ihr seid frei!"—*Drumm girls, come out, you are free!* This entry is dated January 7, 1947, and is written in Irmgard's unmistakable hand.

We were returned to our room after the shower. The next morning, our warden entered the room, and looking in our direction, announced in her usual loud voice,

"Drumm Mädel, kommt 'raus, ihr, seid frei!"

There are events in our lives that have such a momentous impact on us that our whole being is swept up into the experience, leaving our consciousness without any imprint, as it were. This was such a moment for me. To this day, I still have no recollection of this announcement of our freedom, despite all of Irmgard's entreaty, "But don't you remember?" The closest I'm able to come to it is the image of the warden standing a few feet from the door facing us; an incredibly intense feeling—like an explosion of joy, and then light. Some time later, Irmgard captured our reaction in these words:

"I don't know how we felt. I only know that we wept, laughed, stammered disjointedly, our hearts and minds in tangled turmoil. Our joy was boundless."

I then recall us running down the stairs; unable to contain our excitement, oblivious of the warden. She did not stop or reprimand us. In the prison office we found Gerhard and Puka and hugged each other, talking excitedly in spurts as if shaken by inner shivers. I became aware of a figure in the background, looking on quietly and intently. She was wearing the habit of a Methodist deaconess. Her name was Sister Elizabeth; she told us she had come to take us to Prediger Mayr's residence, and later to the home of the Methodist deaconesses in Pötzleinsdorf, a suburb of Vienna.

Then we waited for the release procedure to be completed. Irmgard's name was called, and she stepped up to the clerk's desk while we held our breath, anxious that there might yet be a hitch that would send us back to our cells. But she was only asked to sign a paper acknowledging the return of her personal effects. She was handed her little notebook with the worn, tan cover that she had had to relinquish upon our arrival at the *Rossauer Lände Gefängnis*, which the inspecting warden had categorized as "Klumpert"—*Junk*.

Standing outside the *Rossauer Lände Gefängnis*, the sound of the large wrought iron gate falling shut was a final seal for us that we had, in fact, been set free—that we, at long last, had reached the goal of our journey. It was a journey with many more unexpected turns, hardships, and challenges than our youthful minds ever could have imagined; a journey that would send us into yet another one—an inner journey; one that would serve as a thread of light and reference point.

Taking in this moment—our first steps back into life and the world—we paused. One last glance back, up and along the blackened tall and silent prison walls with its rows of barred windows and no faces that can be seen, then we turned ahead once more. Sister Elisabeth was waiting to lead us up the boulevard where we were to catch a streetcar. As we started out, Gerhard turned to Eduard:

"*Na, Puka. . . ?*"

Puka turned with an expression devoid of all

mockery, and responded: *"JA. Wir sind endlich frei."*— *YES. We are finally free.*

I sat in a streetcar, with Hedy next to me. When I looked up, I looked into Sister Elisabeth's blue eyes. They were vibrant and penetrating, but her gaze was calm.

Soon, we stood at a curbside of a very wide boulevard. Near the opposite side was a narrow island, where passengers boarded and departed on streetcars. We waited to cross to the island. I was stunned by the light and expanse. It was a dazzling, sunny winter day. The sky was a light blue; the distance veiled in a haze of blue-gray. The snow on the streets and rooftops glistened. The rumbling of the subway behind us intermingled with the clamor of streetcars, horns, and the abrupt start and stop of cars and taxis.

People hurried along the boulevard, carrying purses, briefcases, or shopping bags. Some of the faces appeared energetic or expectant, some haunted, while others had resigned expressions. Friends or acquaintances stopped to shake hands, exchange words, and smile as they said goodbye. Others nodded in passing, shouted out, or waved from a passing car. A few muffled figures slowly pulled themselves along the sidewalks; their backs humped as if a weight were pressing down on them. Their faces were turned to the ground—would they ever again be able to straighten their necks and look at the sky, and at things ahead of them? It was all so strange and familiar, close and removed, confounding and incomprehensible.

"Kommt, laufen wir alle schnell hinüber, es ist jetzt sicher!"—*Come, let's all run across, it's now safe!* Sister Elisabeth was calling. Irmgard reached for my hand:

"Dori komm, wir können jetzt hinüber!"—*Dori, come, we can cross now!*

"Yes," I said, and I took her hand.

Family in Pötzleinsdorf, Vienna, 1949. Left to right, front row: Dora, Irmgard, Claudia, Gerhard. Back row: Hedy, Mama, Tata (Father), Eduard.

Passport Photos for Immigration
to the United States, 1949

Hedy

The Winds of Fortress Kula

Irmgard

Gerhard

The Winds of Fortress Kula

Dora

Eduard

It was shortly after noon when Sister Elisabeth pressed the doorbell to Herr and Frau Mayr's second-floor apartment. The door opened, and together they greeted us warmly. I recognized Frau Mayr from the pictures I had seen in my parents' photo albums: first, as a young, unmarried woman in my mother's circle of friends back in the province of Batchka, and later, as the wife of one of my father's colleagues at conference meetings in different cities and countries.

Active and energetic, Frau Mayer had a plan laid out, designed to facilitate our re-entry into society as well as enhance our comfort and appearance. We quickly shed our worn clothes like old skins, and then following her instructions, dropped them into the blazing flames of a well-stoked iron stove. Following a warm, cleansing bath; so soothing that one had to fight the temptation to linger, we, like newborns, were soon dressed in a set of clean clothes; which Frau Mayr had ready for our selection from CARE packages sent by US Methodist donors. Finally, Frau Mayr nourished us with a warm supper—the aroma and flavor reminiscent of our mother's cooking.

Sister Elisabeth had returned to take us to our final destination of the day. Before we had finished taking our leave, Frau Mayr pulled Irmgard aside. She appeared to want to impress something upon her, which had the effect of making our sister look embarrassed. Charged with the responsibility of transmitting Frau Mayr's counsel, Irmgard conveyed that we should not be telling everyone our story, and especially not in vivid detail. For after all, everyone had a war story of their own. Irmgard had taken Frau Mayr's word not only as well-intentioned advice, but also as a reprimand.

We were on our way to Pötzleinsdorf. I was sitting in a streetcar across from Sister Elisabeth. We now knew that she was Herr Mayr's pastoral assistant. The conductor called out "Endstation" in a sing-song tone.

From here we walked up a narrow, cobblestone street. To our left, the street was lined with small, quaint shops; to the right, cottage-like dwellings. Up the slope, the street curved to the right. A friendly, thick-walled chapel stood there like the statue of a benign saint, greeting the passersby, watching over their safe passage. We took a turn before reaching that point, and walked up two narrow flights of stairs between stone masonry walls, past a cemetery on the upper right. We had come to a plateau with a broad vista of the distant city. It was wide and open here. The stillness was broken by the movement of large wings flapping, lifting from tall treetops to glide through the evening sky. After one more turn at the end of the street, we walked along an iron fence and arrived in front of the gate.

In the dusk we glimpsed a large garden stretching down a slope. At the foot, half-hidden by trees, we saw traces of a large, two-story cream-colored villa. Walking down the winding gravel paths, our steps making the same crunching sound as when we walked through the city park back home, we felt as if transported into an enchanted tale. The building now came into full view: a portico resting on solid columns stretched across the wide front of the house. Front and side steps led up to it. Groupings of white French doors spanned the front. Above were two rows of white windows. From the slate roof, dormer windows were looking out. A noble, friendly structure, both holding and reflecting light.

We'd been introduced and warmly welcomed by the other four deaconesses living here. I sensed a certain empathy and regard in their gaze and attitude. After we'd had some tea, the tallest and most robust of the sisters, Sister Andrea, declared:

"Die jungen Leute gehen am besten gleich ins Bett."— *The young folks had best get straight to bed.* A medical nurse by training, she had observed us closely through her small but thick silver-rimmed glasses. We were tired, and eagerly complied with Sister Andrea's suggestion. Thanking our hosts for their hospitality and welcome, we followed her upstairs to our night quarters: two cozy attic rooms. "This one for the brothers and this one for the sisters," she told us. She herself occupied a third room on the same floor, facing the front. Feeling very weary, our brothers went at once to bed.

We sisters were in our room. It felt so peaceful and homelike. A large attic dormer window looked onto a sloping hillside with vegetable beds and fruit trees. On each side was a bed with cloud-like covers, clean linens and large, soft feather pillows. In the luminescence of that hour they appeared as emblems of infinite hope and grace. That we should rest in such comfort again felt unspeakably wonderful and healing.

The End

NOTES

The story of our flight had been gestating inside me for years, urging to be told. Coming upon Irmgard's tattered, small notebook set in motion the momentum to write it. Irmgard had acquired the palm-sized notebook and pencil stub somewhere on our flight. She has no recollection of how or where. What is certain is that she didn't have them with her at the time we escaped from the internment camp. Consequently, Irmgard's sparse, shorthand-like entries only lightly touch on the beginning phase of our flight, and stop with our transport to the prison in Vienna.

Our family was interned twice. The first time was in November of 1944 when the ethnic German citizens of Vršac (1/3rd of the town's population) were interned. Our release shortly thereafter, was brought about by the appeal of the residing Orthodox bishop and two other respected Serbian citizens of Vršac who knew our father and vouched for him and the family. Fourteen months after we were allowed to return to our home, we were interned for a second time. My narrative launches with this second internment.

*Our two oldest sisters, Hildegard and Erika, are not included in my account. They had fled Yugoslavia in September of 1944, just steps ahead of the retreating German army and the advance of the Red Army.

Our indirect route was determined by geographic and political considerations, as well as by ensuing events. Getting beyond Yugoslavian territory and into a neighboring country as quickly as possible was paramount, even if that country was also under communist rule as Romania and Hungary were. The danger of being caught, imprisoned, and deported back to Yugoslavia was real here too, but not as inescapably certain as if we tried to take a direct route through Yugoslavia to Vienna. The latter was, in fact, unthinkable. Given that Vršac was merely a dozen or so miles from the Romanian border, the zig-zag route of fleeing first eastward into Romania, then westward into Hungary, and from there northward into Austria, was the most expedient one for us to take.

Donauschwaben—Danube Swabians refers to the ethnic German population who lived in the northeastern region of former Yugoslavia, western Romania, and southern Hungary. The name refers to the early groups of immigrants (only a small number of them actually from Swabia), who traveled through Swabia and along the Danube river, and settled in the vast central European Plain, known also as the Danube or Hungarian Plain. Large-scale immigration took place in the 18th and early 19th century, but was preceded by smaller ones in the 17th and throughout the 19th century. The precursor was the epochal defeat of the Ottoman Turks by the Habsburg forces and the Emperor's subsequent call to his subjects to colonize and cultivate the repossessed lands. The extraordinary achievement of the Danube Swabian settlers was the transformation of the fertile but malaria- ridden swampland into the breadbasket of Europe.

ACKNOWLEDGEMENTS

I am especially indebted to my sister Irmgard's twenty-five page story, "Unsere Flucht" (1947). She wrote this account in a matter of days, some months after our release in Vienna. Most of my references to her account of our flight, and all quotes, come from her story. The passages included in my narrative have met with her approval, as has my translation of them. I am also indebted to my daughter, Nadine, for her editorial critique of the manuscript, including untangling some of my German-based syntax. I am grateful to my niece, Margaret Drumm, for providing the map of our flight; to my daughter, Krista, for her unfaltering moral support; to my son-in-law, Charles, for his help with the images, and various digital hurdles; and to Christina Kauk for her technical support. Lastly, I wish to express my gratitude to those at Friesen Press: to my editor for her encouragement and editorial attention; to the Publishing Specialists, Galia Zavgorodni, Joshua Robinson, and, not the least, Sarah Mitchell, who guided me through the steps for publication; and to the book designer, Geoff Soch.

ABOUT THE AUTHOR

Dora Van Vranken was born in former Yugoslavia to a fourth-generation ethnic German father and a Hungarian-born mother. She grew up in ethnically-diverse communities, first speaking Hungarian, then German, and upon entering elementary school, Serbian. By age thirteen, she had seen two wars fought in the streets of her hometown of Vršac: Hitler's forces conquering Yugoslavia in 1941, followed by the Russian Red Army liberation in 1944. Both wars left in their wake major upheaval—ethnic tensions and persecutions; hardship and suffering. For Van Vranken, her experience under Tito's Communist rule included internment, separation from her parents and some siblings, forced labor, and a risky escape and flight. Reunited in Vienna, she and her family emigrated in 1949 to the United States, settling in California. Once able to resume her education, Van Vranken pursued Liberal Arts. She holds a Ph.D. from Stanford University in German Studies. As a tenured Professor at University of Redlands, she taught German and other literatures. After retiring, Van Vranken turned to writing. *The Winds Of Fortress Kula* is her first book. Van Vranken lives in the Bay Area to be near her two daughters.

CPSIA information can be obtained
at www.ICGtesting.com
Printed in the USA
BVHW030505140620
581355BV00005B/111